THE TROUT KING

BY
C.E. PICKHARDT
www.carlpickhardt.com

ISBN: 978-1-963565-92-8 (Paperback)
ISBN: 978-1-963565-91-1 (Ebook)

Library of Congress Control Number: 2025903868

Printed in the United States of America

Published by:

info@thequippyquill.com
(302)-295-2278

This is a fishing story so you know it can't be true

To the universal brotherhood of fishermen.

To the craft they practice,

To the luck they serve,

To the love which drives them,

To the hope which sustains them.

May they never stop trying.

May they never give up.

THE TROUT KING
C.E. PICKHARDT

TABLE OF CONTENTS

PROLOGUE
THE HAT

Pulling the dust-covered box out from behind the workbench in the basement where he had paid it no attention over the years, the boy lifted the lid and discovered, scrunched down inside, a funny kind of hat, sheep wool on the top covered with many brightly colored and oddly shaped fishing flies hooked into the fleece.

Lifting the peculiar headgear out for further examination, he noticed the stack of papers lying underneath. Across the top page, written in his grandfather's hand, were the words: "The Trout King." Curious to read more, but not sure he should since it had been stashed away, he put the hat back inside, closed the lid, and carried the box up the cellar stairs in search of the person who could tell him more.

"Gramps," asked the boy of the man who lay lost in an afternoon doze, "what's this?"

The older man blinked, stared at his grandson, sat up, stretched, and rubbed his eyes awake.

"So you found it."

"You thought I would?"

"Yes, you're curious like your dad was, always on the sniff for something new. So, I figured I'd just wait for you to make the discovery. Now that you have, I guess it's time for you to know."

"Know what?"

"About me when I was a much younger man and about your dad at your age. About a father and a son and the fishing adventure they had one summer that forever changed their lives. Hadn't have been for the accident that took him and your mom away, and you come living with us, I believe he would have written about it like he meant to do. When he couldn't, I thought I'd give it a try. He told me once how I had a way with words, as I guess a lot of salesmen do. The writing took some time, piecing things together, some true and a lot made up because I couldn't know it all, not for sure. So, it's told a little roundabout, but that's the best path I could find, skipping from place to place, pretending to get into people's heads and people's lives to lay out the storyline I believe your dad would have wanted to be told."

"And the hat? Is that part of the story?"

"Oh yes. I never fished without it."

"You don't fish anymore."

"No, not anymore. When your dad died, the fishing went out of me. Maybe even before then, when we had to leave Bishop's Place."

"Bishop's Place?"

"Read the story and you'll understand."

"But who is The Trout King?"

"Now that's the riddle the story asks. For what it's worth, I'll give you a hint to help stir up some confusion. Of course, it could be Front, your dad, since he caught the great trout. It could even be me, Sam Henry, because I helped him do it. Then there's the man MacGregor. After all, he retired the title. Or what about Ojay? Without her savvy, neither Front nor MacGregor would have caught their fish. Then there's the Reverend. His cast caught MacGregor into going to church. Or there's your grandmother. Estelle caught Front with her love of reading. What about Wally? It was he who created the contest to become The Trout King in the first place. Even Goeff

MacGregor, because he earned the right to take his father's place. And you have to consider the great trout itself, the king of its kind. Most of all there's the river. No river, no fish, and no fishermen. So, it's up to you to answer your question."

"You're not giving me much help. Where does the story start?'

"The same place every fantastic fishing story begins, with a great fish in deep water maybe waiting to be caught."

CHAPTER ONE

THE GREAT TROUT

Its large unblinking eyes could not see the injured dragonfly drop off an overhanging branch into the rushing water upstream from the pool in which the great trout watched and waited, its heavy body held steady against the strong current by a slight waving of its powerful tail. Intelligence grown wary over years of survival caused the fish to sense even the subtlest disturbance in its surroundings, and to discriminate threat from opportunity, always suspecting the dangerous possibility first.

So when the floundering insect at last floated into view the fish did not immediately attack, but waited for the unusual commotion on the surface of its world to pass, then turned and followed the struggling creature, nudged it, circled underneath and rising slapped it with its tail, paused, and seeing no response but stillness, sucked the drowned thing into its enormous mouth, held it for a moment of final deliberation, then swallowed it down.

No sooner had the urge to feed been satisfied than another took its place: the need to hide. With a burst of speed, the great trout fled for protection under the rock ledge where it habitually lay, invisible to predators that did not live in running water but hunted there for food.

Over the many years since an August flood had washed it, young and inexperienced, down into the deep bend of the river, the fish had grown in caution as well as size until flight was an instantaneous response to any uncertainty; while the pool itself provided perfect sanctuary from all pursuit.

Rushing headlong into a granite wall the river was forced to turn swiftly at right angles along a steep rock face, the current dredging out a deep bottom and, over an indeterminate time, eroding underwater recesses into the unforgiving stone. These were always sheltered from sunlight and guarded by a tangle of broken trees and other debris that spring thaws and late summer rains had caused the swollen stream to deposit there year after year.

The great trout knew this world with the familiarity of one whose life depended upon an intimate knowledge of its surroundings. Those dead trees particularly had served the fish well when it had inexplicably become a victim of its prey, striking to feed only to feel a sudden pull that it violently opposed. Loss of freedom is like death to a wild thing, so the fish had fought with absolute abandon, shaking its thick neck in protest, diving deep and fast and hard, dashing in and out of the sunken branches until captivity was torn from its ragged jaw and something shiny, something colored, nothing that looked any longer like food, hung from the limbs and fluttered limply in the water's flow.

That it was the object of sport the fish did not know, did not know a spinner from a streamer, did not know what fishing was. Survival was all it knew, but it knew that well; while the boy, gazing earnestly upriver from the woods below, wondered how his father would read this pool and where he would place his first cast.

CHAPTER TWO

ENCOUNTER AT THE RIVER

Stepping carefully into the icy water his foot inadvertently rolled one small rock against another making no sound he could hear but immediately startling the great trout, already hidden from the boy's sight, into more complete concealment.

The fly he had selected was his favorite, a gray Parachute -- feather spun out across the top of the hook's shank around a tiny upright piece of twisted aluminum wire, attached there by winds of thread and a drop of glue, finally flattened down with pliers to keep the spreading hackles in place. On both sunny and overcast days it was highly visible and "floated like a boat", as his father, who loved exaggeration, was fond of saying.

Even though the boy knew nymphs and wets and streamers were more productive lures in summer, more imitative of the trout's natural diet at this time of year, he enjoyed the dry fly most of all and so used it against the advice of better judgment and likelihood of better luck. Watching it speed through the air, flutter down to the water, land so lightly and then ride so buoyantly along the current delighted his eyes, while the strike, when it occurred, thrilled him with excitement.

If he had a favorite moment in this sport it was the strike – watching the fly sucked under, attacked on the surface, or most dramatic of all beholding a trout leaping clear of the water and diving down upon the feathered creation of his own hands. Every fly he tied, and he tied only two kinds, the Parachute, and the Bivisible in varying colors, he was always blessed with anticipation that this one fly might just catch the one improbably large trout that he and his father never tired of talking about, but which each knew had no reality except in the love of wishful thinking they both shared.

Although the man throve on competition, there was no sense of contest between them. Only a son striving to learn the craft of fly fishing from the man he believed had mastered it, which his father denied. "No. No experts in this business. Except maybe the trout, but they're not talking. We try, they decide. That's how it works. Using flies just makes our job more complicated." This was what called to the boy, this desire for challenge they both shared and the bond between them it created.

Checking over his shoulder for obstacles behind and waiting for a lull in the breeze that ran down the river between the tall pine trees like a separate river of its own, the boy began waving his rod back and forth, measuring the outline stripped from the reel, releasing it through his fingers at the backward and forward extremities of each cast until, estimating the distance he wanted, he shot the line out slacking it just as the cast uncurled, causing the fly to hover and then alight on a likely looking riffle. For a short moment the fly held still in the swift water, then the line, pulled by the current, began to drag the fly downstream, the boy staring attentively as he recovered the line in short quickly taken loops, keeping the connection between himself and the fly as taut as possible, alert for the unexpected, savoring the suspense of this anticipation, ready to set the hook if luck should strike.

Soon, in a matter of seconds, the fly swept by where he was standing, watching, waiting until the line had almost straightened out when he flicked his wrist and instantly the rod responded, lifting up the fly before it drowned, thrusting it toward a new location, his feet groping forward, another cast begun, another possibility for catching fish created.

The first day on the river rarely yielded any trout. Not that he lacked desire, but his concentration was distracted by observing how the river had been altered over the intervening year. Shallow places had been built with sand and gravel from stretches further up that now ran deeper than before. Collapsed banks with trees uprooted extended horizontally over the water, branches raking the surface creating new hazards for fishermen and new hiding places for the fish. Logs that had seemed permanent fixtures in the past were inexplicably missing. It was too much to notice, too much at one time.

Each summer his first job was to study the river's redesign. He had been told: "Where the trout lay depends on how the river changes and that river is just like you and me. It never stays the same for very long. That's why reading the river is half of what trout fishing is about. The fancy casters with fashionable gear and perfect flies may look impressive but often don't perform up to appearance. No wonder. They can't recognize good holes and cover. You just learn to read the river and you'll do all right." Advice the boy had taken and found true. The technique was tempting, but knowledge caught more trout.

One final cast. His fly swept by the huge rock face without response. No luck today. Time to head back. Reeling in he took a final look upriver then turned to wade for shore, stopping abruptly where he stood. A huge shadow fell between him and the bank, the massive figure of the man who cast it deliberately blocking his path, having stalked the boy in silence and surprised him without warning.

"So, it's vacation time again. Your father with you I suppose?" Towering above him swayed Mr. MacGregor, ill-humored as always.

The boy said nothing as he had been instructed. Nor did he back away. "The man just likes to bully," his father had explained. "But he can't without permission. Don't give him yours."

Seeing the boy unwilling to play at intimidation, MacGregor changed lures, throwing out an insult to see if this would get a rise:

"Here to do your summer poaching, eh? Playing at another man's living. Taking for pleasure is what some of us depend upon for food. That's your way is it?" His way, was to provoke conflict where he could.

Still, no response so MacGregor stung the boy where he knew words could bite: "As for your father, each summer I make sport of sportsmen such as he."

The boy did not like letting criticism of his father go unanswered. 'Drinking a little early today, Mr. MacGregor?' was what he would have liked to say. And more: 'My Dad's twice the fisherman you'll ever be.' But he said neither, suffering the big man's taunts in silence.

"You've not got your father's glib tongue, but you can hear as good as he. So take him this message. Tell Sam Henry the better man is he who catches the biggest trout. And come August I'll be Trout King in Bishop's Place once again. Just as I have each summer past."

The boy nodded. Partly in acceptance of what he had been told to do. Partly in grudging acknowledgment that the boast was true. By whatever means MacGregor used, he had won the local competition every year since it began.

"As for this pool," and here MacGregor spat into the clear water, "I'll give you this advice. It's filled with one thing and one thing only: snags. I've fished it every way for years and come up wanting. So don't waste time casting where there's nothing to be caught." And with this final word of discouragement, the man lurched to the bank and crashed off through the woods, now heedless of the noise that he was making, leaving the boy to slowly wade for shore and head for home, laden with the challenge he was bringing to his father.

The great trout watched him go.

CHAPTER THREE

MAN OF THE HOUSE

Slamming the screen door hard behind him, jarring the frame, MacGregor gave vent to his displeasure:

"Can't a man even get fed in his own house?"

All was in readiness, but he took no notice of the small table dutifully set nor the food kept hot upon the stove awaiting his arrival.

Since the argument would only draw further anger down upon her, Mary did not reply. Silently she placed a boiling pot of potatoes before him and removed the lid, he recoiling from the rising blast of heat as though he'd been attacked.

"Burn me, will you?" He wrenched the cover from her hand scorching his thick fingers on the hot metal, throwing it clattering down to cap the steam.

"You'll kill me one of these days! Then who'll provide? Not yourself!"

But she was busy at the stove turning up the flame, oil popping in the pan, sweet roasted fragrance of fresh trout he'd caught that morning appealing to his appetite as she knew how.

Damn, the woman for being so mysterious! He couldn't figure her out. Never could. Sure of her love one moment, suspecting it the next. Why he generally preferred the company of men. With men, you knew where you stood.

Pushing back in his chair as she approached with the sizzling fish, he distrusted her intent:

"You'll not burn me twice!"

Deliberately he caught her eye, reading disapproval there, receiving it like an insult: "Don't look at me like that!"

Obediently she lowered her glance.

"And don't look away either! As though there's something wrong with me. I won't be judged in my own home!" But judged was how he felt. Not with words. Never with words in over twenty years of marriage. With looks. This look. Of disgust. It made him furious. Had he no right to respect after keeping her in food and shelter, after fathering her sons? What stopped him uttering the question was certainty she would refuse him satisfaction of an answer.

He was correct. The louder he grew the more quiet she would become. He was spoiling for a fight and she knew it. His face was flushed. His blood was up. The smell was on him. In his breath. In his sweat. On his clothes. She could smell the poison in his body poisoning his mood. The sullen signs of drink upon a man. Nothing new. She'd learned to read the warnings before she met MacGregor. Long before. Learned them from men in her own family, good men all except when drink made them go bad. For a while. Until their better half returned sober and sorry for what was said or done if they remembered. If not, at least back to work without complaint no matter the discomfort from the night before. Family men, MacGregor is one of those. Men upon whose industry a wife and children could depend. Resourceful men who always found a way. Untiring, dedicated, entitled to the solace drinking gave. Earning its brief escape from care. Men married to long-suffering, hard-working women who shunned drink themselves or suffered shame if they did not, secretly envying the freedom of intemperance they were denied.

Mary one of these women who learned to endure the drinking of their men without comment but not without censure.

How MacGregor hated her expression of displeasure.

"Well, where are they?" he barked.

"Washing up." Mary was expert at the minimal reply.

"So, I'm to eat at the pleasure of the boys? They can take their time if they like, is that it? Well damned if they'll take mine! Gordie! Goeff! Get in here now or go without! As for you, fetch me another beer while I'm kept waiting."

Mary did as she was bid. Slowly. Her time would come. It always did. Later, when the begging for her pardon would begin. Then for her favors. Apologies and promises began the making up that she initially refused. Whatever power to hurt that he possessed, or possessed him, under the influence of drink was no match for her power to reject repentance that came after. Eventually she would forgive, but at her leisure. And until she did, he was a miserable man. While she was used to his unloving ways, he had no tolerance for hers, immediately in need of reassurance she would take him back. His punishment was fear of losing her after he'd gone too far. A fear that Mary recognized and used, but that struck her as absurd. After over twenty years of marriage where was he thinking she would go?

The boys trundled in wiping wet hands on loose shirt tails, mopping their dripping faces.

"Well, look who's here! The latecomers. The laggers. The two good for nothings. Here to eat off their father's table. Well: what do you have to say for yourselves?"

"We've been about our chores, Da'. Ask Mother if you don't believe me." It was Gordie, the eldest, large like his father, speaking up while Goeff, the younger, half smiled, hung back, and said nothing.

"Chores? And what money did chores bring in? As for your Mother, why she'd lie to protect the likes of you? Isn't that so, woman?" It was an ancient grievance. Blood kin they were to her and he was not. They were her sons while he was her only husband. He never had their power of infancy to elicit bonding love, a tie that made him jealous from the first. So he grudged her with the offense of putting them before himself. Having sons meant the loss of a wife, of her attention, care, and loyalty.   Rivals   for   whom   he   had responsibility. Sons whom he resented and loved, resolving this ambivalence by being hard upon the boys. Challenging them to measure up. Bearing down on them with push and shove, provoking arguments so they could pit themselves against him and grow strong. Which Gordie did. Which Goeff did not.

"We stripped the motor down. Cleaned it and put it back just like you wanted," continued Gordie, determined to prove his father's charges wrong. "But we couldn't get the switch to working in reverse. Only forward."

MacGregor scorned the explanation.

"A job half done? What help is that to me? What good to the customer?"

"None, Da'. But we tried."

"And you, Goeff?" MacGregor wanted to engage the younger boy. "What's your excuse?"

Goeff smiled his half smile, the mask he wore on these occasions, and said nothing. He let his older brother deal with his father.

"I don't hear your reply!" MacGregor's voice now rising with frustration from being ignored. From how this lesser son refused to fight.

Talking to everyone and no on in particular, Mary interrupted: "Here's vegetables. Now eat before they all get cold."

MacGregor felt the chill of her reproof. Could see what disrespect his boys were learning as one son and then the other attacked their plates, obeying Mary, not minding him. No matter how he strove to dominate the family it was she who ruled at home.

But not at work. There MacGregor would suffer no master but himself and himself only barely, being a hard man to work for as Gordie and Goeff discovered early helping out their father. It was understood from the beginning: his livelihood was theirs to learn, his inheritance to them. They were as much indentured to him as they were his sons.

No criticism was the best they could hope for. Compliments never. While one mistake was tolerated and correction brusquely given, two of the same were not. So it behooved both boys to pay attention and catch on as quickly as they could which Gordie did watching his father do it first, Goeff by listening while having it explained. The older boy was instinctively imitative, able to translate another's actions into his own through observation. Yet he could not grasp directions that words alone conveyed and so was considered slow at school, which he was not. They just didn't teach to his strength. Goeff was considered brighter of the two, learning through listening concepts to which his eyes were blind. While MacGregor instructed to the difference, showing Gordie and explaining to Goeff. Why not? So long as they acquired the necessary skills he did not care how acquisition was accomplished. As for school, it had served him ill enough so he expected little better for his sons. However, he took their education seriously enough.

Fathering was a stern responsibility: making men of boys. To this end he taught them what a man should know. To fish, of course, for that was putting meat upon the table. Carpentry and construction. The boys had never lived in a home he had not built or rebuilt by himself. Mechanical repair. He had a gift for figuring from how things worked, how they had broken down. To this was added one gift more: a capacity for rigging, for contriving the unorthodox when ordinary means would not avail.

Self-sufficiency was his religion. A man should manage on his own, do for himself. Requesting help was declaring helplessness. It meant admitting incapacity and worse, incurring expense or obligation. Better to do without than do with help. He would pay the cost of independence and he did, becoming a man of many trades, member of none. Self-educated, he was not certified to do what he did well. Cities, he had tried a few, held this lack of formal training against him, but in the county folk were less particular. They judged a man on his performance not his preparation.

So it had been in Bishop's Place. No one asked where he had come from, what he'd done before. They only noticed his arrival. How could they not? He and Mary with the infant boys in a car repaired beyond recognition of its original manufacture, pulling a trailer rattling behind. The trailer crafted to a double purpose: for working out of and for living in. The man himself, large and loud spoken, stopping in at every business on the street, introducing who he was, making his offer. Give him a try on what they couldn't fix, on what was broken but not thrown away. At his expense. If he succeeded, they should remember MacGregor next time a handy man was needed.

Within a week his reputation was established. Within two he had begun making a living, just in time for the summer trade to take him on, vacationers who came to play and could afford to contract out for work. By fall he had agreed to remain another year. Mary was tired of wandering. She longed for a chance to settle down, to create a home for her family. And she liked the little church, the preacher there. Meeting him by the river, MacGregor liked him too, a man who fished for solitude just like himself, inclined to argue when there was talking to be done. Compatibility welcome to them both.

As for 'settling down', Mary might as well have sentenced him to jail for the entrapment MacGregor felt when she had said it. But the river reminded him of home and meant they would not starve. While the crowd down at the Tavern proved a convivial lot after the first few drinks, although they treated him as an outsider during the day. Until he won their game, became Trout King. Then they acclaimed him for their own so they could share in his reflected glory, could congratulate themselves for the victory he won.

The meal eaten and his evening about to begin, MacGregor announced:

"Sam Henry's back. I caught his son casting at Riverbend. The boys not got the fishing sense of his father, bad luck to them both! I gave him notice for his dad. From the Trout King."

"Have you never caught a fish there, Da'?" asked Gordie for whom MacGregor, drunk or sober, was a hero of a man.

"The answer's in your question: never. Two kinds of luck is what that pool has to offer. Bad and none at all. The water runs too deep and fast for trout to stand the current. I told young Henry. Why not? He'll learn it soon enough himself. Some water's fouled by fortune. Not meant to be fished. The Riverbend is one."

MacGregor pushed himself away from the table with a contented sigh, stood up and stretched, the meal by now having subdued the irritation in his system.

"Come on you two," he gruffly invited. "Before I leave I'll teach you how to fix a switch so next time you won't be troubling me."

The boys followed him outside, Mary watching as they crowded round to see and hear how it was done. Times like this she loved MacGregor for the father he was.   Times without the competition she never understood. Rivalry with his own sons! It made no sense. Treating offspring as enemies. Provoking and confronting, challenging and opposing. For what?

"For what?" she would ask him in the peace and quiet of their laying in bed together late at night when the man would soften as he did to no one else.

"I'm their father, Mary.   Will you never understand? Daughters I could have left to you. But sons? No. Sons are a father's work. Sons must go up against their father if they are to become men. While the father, to remain man of the house, must keep the upper hand."

"And where will it end?" Mary would ask, bewildered.

"By their driving me from my own house, which will never happen, or by themselves being driven out."

But no matter how often he described the path to manhood in his family, sincerely trying to help her understand, Mary could not grasp the natural justice of it all. Even narrating how he himself, after the fight of his life, had been driven from home by his own father to take independence on whatever terms he found it, she could not comprehend.

"Did your father not love you?" To Mary this treatment seemed all wrong.

"Not love me?" asked MacGregor incredulous at the question. "Of course he loved me. Or else he would not have beaten me as he did. He was proud to see me go. And I was proud to leave. Did I not give a good account of myself?"

Mary would shake her head.

"But you treat the boys so angry. And not just the boys. The world."

"Angry? Me? Naw! You should have known Grandfather. Now there was a man who loved his rage. I'm tame compared to him. Even to my father – the only one of the five sons who dared oppose their Da'."

"Why were they so angry, your grandfather and father? What about?" Mary kept searching for the key.

"About?" asked MacGregor as though the question was too obvious to answer. "About nothing. About everything. It didn't matter what. Any grievance would do. Being angry was their way of being men."

It was no use. He was unchangeable. Fixed as a boulder. That indestructible. That strong. Able to meet any adversity. Why she loved him and found him hard to bear. Exacting penance for his domineering ways until, remorseful, he pled forgiveness, urgency for affirmation of her love arousing him to kindness, setting free the gentle language that she loved to hear, the language that he spoke only to her. Then she would make a welcome place for the large man beside her, letting him stir her like the ocean, he the waves breaking upon her again and again 'til he stopped rocking and they grew calm, spent and at peace. Then the confiding with each other would begin, sharing stray bits and pieces of themselves, at last sweet sleep together after they were done. All wrongs righted. All troubles forgot. Tomorrow a new beginning.

Thanking God for this gift of sexual reconciliation, Mary offered up a prayer of gratitude. And then another prayer of hope: "May this connection between us never be broken."

CHAPTER FOUR

TYING FLIES BY NIGHT

"Francis John Henry! When I tell you to be back by six o'clock, I don't mean six thirty, you hear? And no excuses! We didn't give you freedom on the river so we could worry when you're late." As usual, Estelle's anxiety came out as anger.

"Your mother's right, Front. I was about to look for you myself. Did you run into trouble?" Sam's response to any fear was to take action.

"No. Only Mr. MacGregor. He wouldn't let me pass until he'd given me his message." Front was patient with his parents' disapproval, grateful they could at least agree on that.

"And when he did?" Sam was curious to hear what his summer rival had to say.

Front told his parents word for word.

"Sam, I don't trust the man. I never have. He could be dangerous."

"Now Stel, don't make too much of Mac. He's mostly brag and swagger. Besides, it's me he's after. Not Front. We just like to gig each other, nothing more. Don't take him seriously."

"Then don't you take him lightly?"

"Stel, I tell you there's no harm in the man."

"Sam, suppose there is?"

"Stel, I fish against the man. I ought to know!"

"Oh, what's the use!"

Frustration for them both. Another idle conversation ended up in conflict. One more difference of opinion is unresolved. Discouraging for Front, how they could love him so much easier than they could love each other. Turning away he shrugged his sadness off as he had learned to do. Noticing, his parents felt a stab of sadness too.

The argument was abandoned, they sat down silently to eat, shadow settling around the small stone house as the sunlight fell behind the mountains and the valley filled with dusk, soon darkening tonight.

Hot enough to swim during the day, it grew cold enough by evening to build a fire by which, after supper, Front's mother sat and read. Summer her time for reading, while he and his father tied flies at adjacent tables under the glare of an old standing cast iron lamp planted on the floor between them.

Early in his apprenticeship, Front had decided two kinds of flies were all he'd learn to tie, varying the colors of fancy moved him, keeping the task as simple as possible, still catching fish with what he made. His father on the other hand never tired of experimenting with original designs.

"Part of the challenge and the fun," he had explained, "is to keep creating ways to tempt a trout." This was Sam: always figuring. Always in the market for a new idea.

Preoccupied with separate involvements, father and son drifted in and out of conversation, content in their own and each other's company, while Estelle immersed herself in a world of fiction, in love with tales writers had to tell, biding her time 'til she could catch the interest of her son, could initiate him into the literature she loved to teach. No hope for Sam on whom she finally had given up, he was as disinclined to read as she was to fish.

"There. This ought to stir some interest," announced Sam freeing a finished fly from the vise and holding it out for his son's examination.

"What's it supposed to be?" asked Front, genuinely puzzled.

"A helgrammite. Worm-like insect with lots of legs. Some people use them as bait for bass. I'm going to get the trout's opinion of it tomorrow. One rule in this business: the customer knows best."

As much as he respected his father's inventiveness with flies Front envied the man's easy way with words. At an awkward age for self-expression, the boy talked little and listened much, which encouraged Sam to talk more, although encouragement was not needed. A natural conversationalist with a gift for banter, and an entertaining storyteller, Sam put these skills to use in his profession.

If certain men are born to sell, Sam Henry was one. Sell what? It didn't matter. As long as the product was an honest answer to a legitimate need. These two conditions met, he had the impetus to gladly go about his work – offering the public an opportunity from which both he and they could profit. If they refused, the loss was theirs. Although not permanent because he did not close the door on those who closed the door on him, promising he would return after allowing time for them to reconsider, which they often did because Sam did not believe in giving up. Persistence was his discipline of choice, while the challenge of overcoming sales resistance was as irresistible as competing against rivals in the marketplace. Sales was a service in which he believed and a game he loved to play. Hard to refuse a man who so thoroughly enjoyed his calling.

A man of his word. A trustworthy man. A man endowed with the power to convince. A persuasive man himself was persuaded that what he had to sell was good for others. A man who dwelled on the light side of life and made light of the dark. Whose sense of humor kept him in good humor, expecting good, extracting good from bad when it occurred. A man who had chosen optimism to live by because its opposite held no emotional allure. Why be downcast when one could choose to feel uplifted? Positivism was his religion and he would listen to no one who preached obedient suffering or countenanced despair. As happy to make a new contact as he was to greet an old customer, Sam Henry was a pleasure to know, the pleasure of his company was part of what he had to sell as well. Hard to tell which was his work and which his recreation, selling or fishing, since long ago they merged in his mind, each used as a metaphor to describe the other – fishing for prospects, prospecting for fish.

"But if you don't get a strike on this new fly, you won't throw it away," argued Front, knowing his father kept tackle boxes filled with copies of every fly the man had made, the boy wishing he had such a collection.

"Oh no. That's another rule: never give up on a fly no matter how roundly it's rejected. The customer may always be right, but his tastes keep changing. And what turns away one customer may attract another. No accounting for tastes in this business."

Feeling diminished by comparison, Front confessed:

"Except when we fish together and you give me some of yours, I only use the kinds I tie."

"Nothing to be ashamed of," corrected his father. "Probably the better part of wisdom. You know those flies will produce because they have before. That confidence is awfully important. All fishing is an act of faith. Got to be. Never make a fly you don't believe in. Never cast one out you don't expect to catch a fish. Don't feel shy about using what you have faith in. I'm a salesman and I know. Make my living talking other people into buying what I believe they need. Part of what they buy is my belief. Lose that and I start losing customers."

"Do you believe you'll be Trout King this summer?" asked Front, deliberately testing his father's confidence on a matter close to home.

"Yes. Each summer I give MacGregor a stronger run for his money. Last year I almost had him and he knew it. This year I'm going to give it everything I've got. Of course, he's not your usual fisherman. More of a hunter really. A hunter who happens to kill trout. Comes from a long line of poachers, does MacGregor. Meat fishermen who've devised more ways to filch trout from their hiding places than you or I can imagine. Early days, his people wove line out of horsehair and crafted poles from saplings. Even bent their own hooks. Trespassed private property to claim their due. Fought running battles with game wardens to keep from getting caught. Beat MacGregor? Nothing I'd love better because nothing I hate worse than losing like I've lost to him and he knows it. That's why he spoke to you the way he did -- to rub it in. But this year I'm loaded with fresh ammunition. I tied lots of flies last winter. They're my edge. My inventiveness against his resourcefulness. No holding back from battle. This time it's do or die."

The boy couldn't help smiling when he recollected some of his father's more elaborate designs, particularly the ones Sam used to decorate his fishing hat, an act of costuming that exaggerated the man's appearance in a comical way. The crown was solid sheepskin, fleece facing out, attached to a circular brim of stiffened canvas. Into the wool were hooked a great variety of garish-colored and oddly shaped flies that the boy assumed were for purposes of decoration only. Certainly, no one would actually fish with such absurdities. To Front, the helgrammite, with its spiny legs and segmented body, seemed weird enough to join this outlandish collection that his father habitually wore.

"Maybe you ought to add that one to your hat," he suggested pointing to Sam's most recent creation. "It doesn't look like anything a trout would recognize."

The man reached behind him and from on top of his creel withdrew the sacred headgear which he fished in rain or shine.

"I suppose you think these are just for show?" he asked.

The boy nodded.

"Well, they are. Mainly. But they're also for emergencies. For times when nothing is working so anything is worth trying. These are my Outrageous Flies."

"Outrageous Flies?" Front had never heard the term before.

"Yes. Take this one, for instance." Sam pulled from the sheepskin a bright red and blue example that seemed to combine the slender properties of a streamer with the stubby ones of a popping bug.

"What do you call it?" Front wanted a name.

"I don't know. Yes, I do. We'll name it the Desperation Special. I tried it late one night several winters ago when summer felt very far away. Dreamed it up to catch the fish of my dreams. I must say, the few times I've tried it the commotion has been something terrific. Casts like a barbell and lands like a bomb. The tail wags back and forth like the hind end of a happy dog while the head splashes up waves the size of breakers as you jerk it through the water. The one thing a fish can't do with the Desperation Special is ignore it."

"So it does work?" Front persisted.

"Not so far. But who knows? My personal belief is it will either scare every fish into the next county or else so paralyze them with fear I'll just be able to wade in and scoop them up with my net." Sam was enjoying his flight of fantasy, while Front, although entertained, wanted the truth.

"Have you ever really caught anything on an Outrageous Fly?"

"Never," his father admitted. "But that's not to say I couldn't. They have always been a last hope, and no fisherman can afford to be without one of them. Matter of fact, when a fisherman loses hope he generally loses interest in fishing. No such thing as a pessimistic fisherman in this world. At least not for long." And Sam snapped a fresh hook into his vise, with a few loops of thread attaching the bobbin which swung back and forth underneath marking time until the man decided what manner of invention to tie up next.

The boy listened with a mixture of skepticism and belief. Sometimes it was hard to trust his father's meaning. Truth and fiction were so often tangled up in what he said. Like the Outrageous Fly. Truly an improbable idea. And he said so.

"Oh I don't know," countered Sam. "Fly fishing has always been part sense and nonsense. The Outrageous Fly just pushes the limits, that's all. It's an odd notion to begin with, fly fishing. You and I throwing out feathers as imitation food to trout who should know better. But we do and they don't and it works. So now we have a matter of degree. The principle is silly but the practice is sound. Maybe it takes Outrageous Flies to catch Outrageous Fish."

"Like an enormous brown trout, you mean?" added Front alluding to the fish his father prized the most.

"Yes. One of these days. One of these days, if Luck looks my way, I'm going to tie into the defending champion brown trout for the battle of my life. Or his, if I win. Pull against tug, his tricks against mine, with only the strength of a leader to decide the outcome between us. May the smartest one prevail!"

"You mean the strongest," corrected Front.

"No. I mean what I said. The bigger they grow the more subtle they become. Why they'll suck your fly in so gently you'll think it's no more than a swirl in the current. And by the time you've discovered your mistake they will have discovered theirs and spit it out and disappeared. Even if you do manage to hook one, he'll have a dozen ways to break your line. And your heart. I know. Smartest and the biggest, the Brown. Brought over to this country years ago from Europe and like other immigrants ended up on top of the heap."

"Like Mr. MacGregor?" asked Front.

Sam smiled. "I never thought of him that way. Yes, you could say so. A special breed of fisherman. Not out for pleasure like you or I. More of a predator is Mac, the trout his natural prey. Once, years ago before the contest came between us, he took me with him on the river. There was a lesson to remember. Like trying to learn to hunt from a tiger. Instructional, but education is no substitute for instinct. I've never seen such eyes. You'd swear he saw beneath the surface of the water. He could spot a feeding fish where I never glimpsed a sign of life. Then bang, his cast, quick as a reflex, like a shot, right on the mark. And he didn't miss a strike or waste time playing what he pulled in. Right then was when I knew I'd never best MacGregor without an edge, inventing flies the only one I had. So ever since I've pushed the limits of design – all the way to my Outrageous Flies."

"But you're not the only competition he has."

"No. There's Ojay. The most productive of us all. Frequency is the best fisherman and she never misses a day. And the Reverend, of course. He only ties into a good one every now and then, but his casting is poetry in motion. It's the beauty of the sport he loves more than catching fish. But I'm the one who gives MacGregor worry because the more I lose the more I want to win, and he knows it."

"But winning isn't why you love to fish."

"No. Winning's why I'd love to beat MacGregor. Fishing is for sport."

"Not for the trout," interjected Estelle as she occasionally did when fishing talk grew tiresome. "I wonder how you'd feel about fishing if trout screamed before they died? At least in hunting the animals not made to suffer."

"At least the fish is given a sporting chance," replied Sam. This was another disagreement that they'd had before. "No, Stel, there's more to fishing than hunting. Shooting the animal, hunters get to do all the attacking. Fishing is trickier. You must entice the fish into attacking first. Then comes the hard part – playing them in. As much opportunity to lose the fish as you have a line to cast out. Hunting? Pull the trigger and it's over. Dead animals don't fight. You miss the challenge, Stel, you really do."

Unpersuaded, Estelle withdrew beyond the reach of argument back into reading, while Front felt torn by their division deep within himself. He wished he didn't. It saddened him for her to disapprove of what he adored. And yet, he knew he had her blessing just the same.

This was true. Although opposed to the recreational killing of fellow creatures, she loved father and son having this bond between them, accepting her role as the odd parent out, the lone woman in a male household, with a son becoming more like his father every day.

"It's not as easy as you think, Mom. The fish don't always bite. Most times they don't." He wished he could convince her over to his side.

Sam lent his support. "Front's right, Stel. Fishing can be as hard on fisherman as it is on fish."

Estelle just shook her head. She and her husband had become so different.

Sam turned to Front. "Like that dry spell last summer. Do you remember?"

Front remembered.

"Almost three weeks without a rise," Sam continued. "Some tough fishing. They rejected everything we had to offer. Thought I might lose you to discouragement, dragging home empty-handed one day, dragging through the next and the next with no sign of trout much less a strike."

"I know. I really felt I earned my luck when it came back." This had been the hardest fishing Front had known.

"You earned something, all right, but no luck. The August rain came to our rescue. Cooled off the air, stirred up the river and we were back in business. Self-respect for not giving up is what you earned. Up to then, I wasn't sure if you had the makings of a fisherman over the long haul. Afterward, I was."

"You never said anything about it. How come?" asked Front.

"Didn't figure I should," replied his father. "Either you were going to stick with it or you weren't. Encouragement from me would only have gotten in the way of you deciding for yourself. I will confess to you now, however, it was a sadness to me. The possibility of losing my fishing companion."

"I'm still here," said Front feeling good about himself.

"You are. And I'm glad. And it's getting late," said Sam. "If each of us is going to get an early start tomorrow morning we'd better call it a night."

Front agreed, arose, stretched his arms, and yawned.

"Want a story?" asked Estelle as she did every night before he went to bed. But he was too excited and too tired.

"Not tonight, Mom. Thanks." And he followed his father out.

She watched him leave. No luck tonight. The timing was everything. Patience in listening to a story depended on his mood. So she slipped back into the uninterrupted reading that she loved, that teaching and grading papers made so scarce during the school year. But her attention was distracted because her mind was ill at ease. Still bothered by Front's encounter with Mr. MacGregor, she wished her husband had been bothered by it too.

CHAPTER FIVE

TWO RIVALS MEET

The Bishop doesn't come here anymore. Only stories of his summer visits remain: how the vigorous old prelate would lead a reluctant entourage north to the mountains to get back to nature and escape the city heat in this cool valley, in this clear river where, if local legend is correct, he refreshed his body and renewed his spirit each morning by plunging naked into the icy mountain stream.

A man of robust constitution and adventurous disposition, the rugged outdoor life suited him far better than it did his followers who finally prevailed upon him to build some permanent encampment for their comfort, if not for his. So a lodge was erected, expanding in size and amenities over the years, requiring for construction and maintenance enough seasonal employment to populate a temporary compound that took root and gradually grew into a town taking for its name the cause of its creation, "Bishop's Place."

By the time the Bishop ceased his visits, the town had gained a modest reputation as a vacation retreat for those with the means to afford it, other summer tourists sustaining the trade that he had started. An unelaborate town, small businesses all fronting on a single street, none of them competing because the town was too small to afford the luxury of competition. So there was only one general store: Detmer's Dry Goods and Grocery.

Cora and Wally Detmer were the proprietors, her parents the original owners now retired from responsibility but not from residence. Mr. was usually found rocking on the porch scouting for customers while Mrs. retained her traditional perch behind the old cash register, greeting folks when they entered and complimenting their purchases when they left. Both parents actually kept watch over the running of the business they built up from scratch to make sure their children did not run it down. Reluctant to let the fruition of a lifetime's labor go, they realized in their seventies it must be passed on before they passed on. Distrustful of this younger generation (nothing personal against Cora and Wally whom they love) these youngsters in their fifties have never known what it was like to struggle except by hearsay. From stories of way back when that have become more romantically unreal the more they have been told, myths of a bygone age perpetuated one generation to the next in the name of history, Mr. and Mrs. Detmer soon to vanish into history themselves, wanting their life work carried on. Confident in Cora and Wally, but worried they have not taught the kids enough and so remind them daily of what they've taught before. The kids, patient out of respect, sharing suppressed irritation only with each other, wishing her parents could leave them alone for a while, then realizing time would soon take care of this, immediately regretting their wish, becoming grateful for the irritation.

Actually, Mr. and Mrs. Detmer need not have worried. Cora was completely in control. Keeping a running inventory in her head, she continually updated it by patrolling the aisles, scanning the shelves, enumerating current stock, and entering altered totals in her strict accounting, accurate to a penny when ringing up receipts before closing each night. The woman had a ledger for a mind. A capacity she took for granted. Not the one that made her proud – never buying anything that did not sell, never discounting any item to move it out. Her suppliers had long ago stopped urging products whose chief virtue was being new. She only stocked the tried and tested. Would not experiment with fads. The reward did not justify the risk.

Sure things were what she wanted, why she married Wally. His loyalty was more important than ambition. He was someone reliable with whom to learn to run the store. The kind of partner who wouldn't quit until whatever needed doing got done. A perfect choice, Wally had never failed her. Slow but steady. And he didn't complain. Like her, he liked keeping busy. Unlike her, he occasionally liked to try out new ideas. Not big ones. The small kind that broke routine enough to create variety. He liked variety, but she distrusted it and objected at first until she came to understand him better and appreciate how a small change made a big difference in his attitude. "Freshened him up", she described it. Reinvigorated him for work.

So it was his idea to have a fishing contest. Arouse some local interest during the heat of summer when enthusiasm naturally lagged. Use the contest as a pretext for bringing people to the store to find out which fisherman was in the lead, to see the actual fish frozen on display. They could read the chalkboard describing the details – who caught it, when, on what, in which part of the river, its length and weight. To come in and share some gossip, maybe buy a little something on the way out.

Eight years ago the idea was frivolous enough to make it fun. But now the contest had grown into something more serious than Wally had intended, a championship the community had come to care about, dividing Bishop's Place along antagonistic lines – pitting locals against summer tourists whose vacation business tided residents over the slow, cold time of the year. Those who had the money to spend sustained those who needed money to live.

August 22, at noon, marked the end of competition. A crowd would gather outside of Detmer's to witness the coronation of the winner in a ceremony having now developed certain traditions, as ceremonies do, incrementally, as people suggested to Wally adornments and formalities to give the proceedings dignity and color, to make it memorable. Most important was a title befitting the victor: "The Trout King."

So far one of the town's own, MacGregor, had carried the day. Each year he reaffirmed native superiority over visitors, a matter jokingly boasted about but seriously meant, a peg upon which community pride could be hung, pride that had turned MacGregor's reputation in Bishop's Place from a braggart to a man with actions to back up his words.

He was a fisherman with only two local rivals, Ojay and the Reverend, both of whom joined the event more to support the town than to try and beat MacGregor, although each was good enough to be competitive. Sam Henry was the one serious contender, an outsider who last year overtook the lead and threatened victory until MacGregor, as though he'd been feeding and breeding his own private stock of lunkers, produced a larger trout on the last day.

There had been great excitement and drinks all around The Tavern to hear MacGregor proudly regale admirers with testimony to his prowess and accept toasts to the countryman who once again had put city folk to shame. Reason enough for celebration, although for Tavern regulars the outcome of the contest made no difference, since win or lose they would have cause to drink.

All in all, it was a great day for the town, an occasion grown greater each succeeding year, a wooden plaque now mounted above the freezer at Detmer's, inscribed brass plates immortalizing each winner's name, each name the same so far. All this from Wally's good idea which until its worth was proven, was no more than a harebrained scheme in the eyes of some, like Mr. and Mrs. Detmer from whom Cora had learned her suspicion of change.

They had come as indirectly close to criticizing Wally at the beginning as they ever dared by asking after the first competition if there was to be a second the following summer, their question implying hope there wouldn't and disapproval of the project as a waste of valuable time. However, dodging the question by deferring to Cora, Wally submitted his creation to her financial scrutiny. To their and her surprise, trade showed a swell in summer business in excess of six hundred dollars, much of it in snacks purchased by people coming in to see who was ahead and admire the winning entry of the moment. Apparently, curiosity sold. Enough said. Issue dropped. Wally rose dramatically in his in-laws' esteem. Both agreed: "There's more going on in that boy than you'd first suppose." Actually, there wasn't. Wally had just accidentally happened on a profitable idea.

Mr. Detmer looked up: "Mr. Henry! Good to see you! Good to have you back among us. The summer wouldn't be complete without you."

Sam grasped the hand held out in greeting, sincerely shaking it because he knew it was sincerely meant, not just a courtesy to welcome the return of summer business. Genuine friendship was extended to him across the line that usually separated Town from Trade, but let Sam Henry in because he was too sociable to let social distance keep him out.

"Well Mr. D, this is going to be my year. I can feel it. Tied me some flies last winter no right thinking, trout will be able to resist.

You see MacGregor before I do, you tell him to start looking over his shoulder 'cause I won't be far behind." Jokingly spoken, but Sam was also serving notice.

Mr. Detmer laughed. "Saw Mac this morning early on his way in from the river. Told me you'd arrived. Told me to tell you, that if I saw you first, he's got something waiting for you in the freezer. Wally! Wally, show Mr. Henry MacGregor's fish."

Wally ambled out and ushered Sam inside where, through the cold glass window, Sam saw the rainbow, three pounds of solid silver, still imposing even in death.

"Some kind of fish, Wally," Sam said in admiration, then looked up at the chalkboard to read where it was caught – the Railroad Shallows, on what – live bait, the kind unspecified because MacGregor was not a man to share his secrets.

"Not bad for openers. He's got my work cut out for me. But the summer's young and MacGregor can't have all the luck."

"Oh can't he?" boomed a deep voice Sam recognized at once.

"Of course, Wally," Sam pretending he had not heard the new arrival, "A three-pound rainbow is pretty fair for those who can't catch any larger."

Now MacGregor shouldered his way in between:

"Larger is it? Larger? Here Wally, weigh and measure this for Mr. Henry," and the big man slid a brook trout still alive with color onto the scales.

Wally waited patiently until the pointer steadied on the mark:

"Almost four pounds, Mac. You've gone and beaten yourself!"

"And who else is man enough to beat me but myself?" asked MacGregor of Wally, but really of Sam who grinned with pleasure at the challenge.

"Nice fish, Mac," said Sam examining the trout more closely, noticing the throat pulled up into the creature's mouth, the gills still bleeding. "Looks like he swallowed the hook."

"And why not?" MacGregor stiffened at the implication.

Sam seemed unaware of the response he had provoked.

"Yes, give a big trout long enough to chew a bait and sometimes he'll do that. Unusual though. Unless you leave it in for quite a while. Like overnight."

"Are you accusing me of setting lines, Sam?"

"Just admiring your trout, Mac. And speculating."

MacGregor shrugged. "Well, words are cheap enough. Better it if you can!" Turning to Wally: "Change my numbers on the board. Freeze this after I gut him. I'll take the rainbow home. As for you, Sam Henry, don't expect to seriously compete at a sport you only play part-time."

"Watch yourself, Mac. Year-round fishing is against the law, you know. Advertise it and you're liable to get fined for angling out of season."

"Bah! All seasons are alike to me. The law? Laws are only meant for those too tame to break them!"

"Speaking for yourself or your ancestry, Mac?"

"For the both, Sam Henry, and don't you forget it! Why I've more cunning bred into me by generations of my kind than you've lifetime to learn."

"True," agreed Sam. "But we both know learning only counts for half of what we catch. The greater half is up to Lady Luck. She'll have the final say between us."

"Luck? Luck be damned! Get born with luck against you and you learn to make your own. Until you know that, your kind won't ever beat the likes of mine." Sooner or later Sam's good sense of humor turned MacGregor's bad.

"Come on, Mac," Wally intervened. "Come on out back and clean your fish so I can freeze it."

MacGregor glared at Sam whose complacency was undisturbed by the argument between them, who suddenly remembered something he wanted to say.

"See here, Mac," the play gone out of Sam's voice, "You meet my son on the river, you leave him alone. He's not for badgering like we do each other."

"I only gave the boy a message, nothing more," grumbled MacGregor.

"And the bluster that went with it. When you have something to tell me, Mac, tell me yourself."

"I treated him no different than my own. I'm a strongly spoken man. My sons will tell you."

"Gordie and Goeff are your business. Front is mine. Mac, let him be."

Seeing Sam's challenge was no longer a sporting one, MacGregor let the matter pass. "Come on Wally. Vacation for some is no vacation for me. I've got work to do."

Sam watched him crowd the exit, barely fitting through the door, then relaxed into his usual good humor, turning now to greet Mrs. Detmer.

"Mrs. D, I see you haven't deserted your station."

"No, Mr. Henry. Been sitting here too long to sit still anywhere else. How's Mrs. Henry and the boy?"

"Fine. Fine. We just pulled in yesterday afternoon. Drove up from the city just like the old Bishop used to do. Except his horsepower was the real thing."

"Before my time, Mr. Henry. Before my time."

"Yes. But in time to hear about the old gentleman first hand."

Recollection caused Mrs. Detmer to shake her head. "Oh, he was a conservation starter. No need to make up stories about him. Lived by his own set of rules, he did. At least during the summer. I suppose he really was a Bishop in the off-season, but to tell the truth, some of his antics make me doubt what I've been told."

"Faith, Mrs. D. Faith. The Church has many mysteries. Perhaps the Bishop, he was one."

"Maybe so. Can I help find what you need?" Mrs. Detmer's sharp eyes had not missed the shopping list stuffed into Sam's shirt pocket.

"I'll holler if I get lost," Sam smiled, knowing he had been instructed to stop talking and start buying. Coming around the second aisle he met Cora. She wasted no time socializing.

"Sam! I heard you come in. Can I get you a phone installed this summer?"

Her question hadn't changed this year any more than his answer.

"No thanks, Cora. Being unreachable is what vacation is about. They'll have to carry one without me."

"You never know about emergencies, Sam. When one might come up."

"In my job, every other call is an emergency. That's why I want to get away. But I appreciate the offer."

"Just thought I'd ask."

"Glad you did. See your folks are doing well. And Wally. But you've reorganized the shelves." And Cora fell to showing him around.

On his way out Sam was detained by Mr. Detmer wanting a word.

"Mr. Henry. It's not my business to meddle in yours, but I wouldn't push MacGregor too hard nor take him too lightly. Him being the Trout King, I mean."

"Why Mr. D. I don't push Mac any harder than he pushes me. As for him being the Trout King, that was last summer. And not by much. His brown outweighed mine by a quarter pound, of all luck!"

"I remember. He was a surly man for most of August, was MacGregor, you leading him down the stretch. Here's what I mean to say. What's game for you may not be game for him. Not anymore. He wins and you're no worse for losing. But you win, and MacGregor comes down hard."

"Are you advising me to leave him a clear field, Mr. D?" Sam was surprised.

"No. No, Mr. Henry. Only asking you to be mindful. Remember how MacGregor is. Too quarrelsome to easily make friends, he's had to earn respect to overcome dislike. And he has. The hard way. With reputation. Local Champion. Trout King. Call him what you will. But there's a price. Each year he wins just gives him more to lose the next."

"And to lose his title is to lose his place?"

"Mr. Detmer nodded. "Win the contest, Mr. Henry, and you make an enemy of the man."

Sam shook his head. While he appreciated the warning confided to him, he could not bring himself to believe it.

"Mr. D, I make my living competing against other men for money. At stake is more than catching fish. Beat or get beaten. There are no split commissions. Only one salesman wins an account. And then to keep it, you've got to fight the others off. But win or lose, I haven't made an enemy yet. And I certainly don't plan to start on my vacation. MacGregor can take his lumps. God knows I've taken mine. But thanks for thinking of me. Now I better get those groceries home before they spoil."

His concern turned aside as a compliment refused, Mr. Detmer felt disappointed. More than that. There was something he had been trying to communicate. Some vague sense of danger. If only Sam Henry lived here year round he might understand. The contest was no longer what it used to be, a simple sporting proposition. Back to Wally. Wally and his good idea might have a lot of bad to answer for.

CHAPTER SIX

A CHANGING OF THE LEAD

"I hate it when the rich people come back to town. Why should they have it easy while we have it hard? I hate the summer!"

It was Goeff who spoke, and the grievance he expressed was deeply felt. Resentful like his father, he was quick to take offense and could mix insult with self-pity and rage at the injustice of it all. Although, unlike his father, he kept his brooding anger hidden except on those rare occasions when bitterness was more than he could swallow and he must spit the venom out, as he did now to his older brother.

"When I grow up I'm going to leave Bishop's Place. I won't come back until I own a summer house and can vacation just like them!"

Gordie shook his head. He did not understand. He loved the town. He loved life. He had no desire to leave. No discontent with living as he did. His father's way was good enough for him. And like his mother, comfort came from settling down.

"Naw, Goeff, It's summer folk who provide most of Da's work. Be grateful they have the money for his hire."

Goeff did not reply but coughed to clear a sticking in his throat. Just released from morning chores, they were wandering the river for an hour of freedom before resuming work MacGregor left behind for them to do.

"Who's that?" Gordie's sharp eyes discriminated between the waving branches of a fishing rod dispensing line. While both could fish because they had been rigorously taught, duress of the instruction had taken any pleasure from the sport. Besides, their father was the Trout King and neither felt he could compete with that.

"It's Sam Henry's son," Goeff felt a sour taste rise in his mouth. "Bet you can't hit him with a stone from here."

Ever one to accept a direct challenge and exceed it if he could, Gordie unwittingly did his brother's bidding. "Oh yeah? Bet I can hit him three out of five."

Goeff smiled to see Gordie take the bait. While he was no match for the older boy physically, Goeff more than held his own by using strategy to outsmart strength.

Stooping to pick up ammunition then moving clear of trees to get an unobstructed shot, Gordie unleashed a fusillade of stone that rained like hail about the unsuspecting victim who quickly recovered from surprise and fled to the opposing bank. Goeff, now feeling free to join the fight his brother started, threw a few rocks of his own. He wanted in but as a follower of a leader who would take the blame.

Like most boyhood fights, this didn't last much longer than the telling takes, all three honorably bloodied for their efforts, each able to make some claim to victory. Gordie and Goeff congratulated one another after repelling Front's counterattack. Front waiting to give his version when he got home.

Sam was first to greet Front and so first to notice the bruises, some still bleeding down his face. Estelle, sensing injury before she saw it, rushed past her husband.

"Front! What happened? You're all cut and scraped!"

"It's all right, Mom. I just slipped climbing down a bank. Fell on my face. It's not as bad as it looks. I'll get cleaned up."

"I'll help you," she offered. "Come to the bathroom where I can wash you off."

"I can do it, Mom!"

Estelle looked to Sam for advice, something she did more frequently now that her son was growing into manhood and his path was sexually unfamiliar.

Sam signed to let the boy attend to his own wounds.

"Can't you get him to be more careful, Sam? He could have been seriously hurt." She wished the man had taught their son more caution, while he believed boyhood was meant for taking risks.

"I'll talk to him." And Sam followed the sound of bathing to where his son was bending over the sink splashing water on his cheeks and forehead, wincing from the sting.

"How do the other guys look?" Sam knew better than to take clear evidence of a fight for an accident.

Front tried to smile. It hurt. "They look as bad as me. One looks worse."

"Tell me about it."

And Front did, confident his father would keep the secret to himself. After all, how could someone who did not believe in violence like his mother appreciate the necessity of fighting growing up? He did not seek it, but when it came his way he did not shy from joining in. Interested, his father sat on the edge of the bathtub while Front described what had occurred at the river, narrating the event as his father would, like a story.

He had been stalking a long quiet pool in search of rises, readying his cast, when one loud splash and then a second broke the silence he was trying to preserve. Not fish breaking but rocks being thrown, one hitting him on the shoulder, one glancing off his neck, another off his cheek, wounds fastening his attention on the throwers – two boys, his own age and a few years older, making sport of him from the bank. Mr. MacGregor's sons, Gordie and Goeff. He recognized them from their scowls whenever they had met. They did not like him. He did not know why. But they were not scowling now, smiling as they hurled their missiles, yelling in triumph when they scored a hit. Ducking and dodging he waded quickly to the other bank.

"Francis! Francis! What you got in your pantses?" The older boy grins with cleverness.

Slow to anger, but quick to ignite once he got there, Front had thrown down his rod, furiously grabbing up rocks from the ground, ignoring the stones pelting his body, hitting their mark because his enemies were country sharp. His pockets fully loaded and cradling what more he could carry in the crook of his left arm, he had charged across the water throwing as he ran, anger inspiring his aim.

Their smiling faces were the targets of his shots, their smiles the bull's eyes he was after. Closing the distance, his accuracy had improved, a smear of red changing the older boy's expression as he grabbed his mouth in surprise, and lowered his hand into a fist only to have the unguarded wound struck a second time, both brothers now falling back before this unexpected onslaught.

Then the tide of battle turned. Out of ammunition and outnumbered by opponents eager for revenge, Front had been driven back across the river but not pursued when they saw him loading up once more, leaving him to ponder what they had meant to prove. Fishing in peace upon the river was up to them, not up to him.

Sam listened gravely, weighing the account of himself that Front had given, on balance proud of his son for holding his own.

"Do you want me to speak to MacGregor? He'd put a stop to it at once. Problems with summer people are problems for business, and he wouldn't want that."

"No," Front replied. "They may leave me alone after today. Goeff was only into it half-hearted. It was Gordie who led him on. I split his lip. They didn't get the fun they wanted."

"Sounds like they'll have explaining of their own to do," observed Sam. And he was right.

Sure enough, they did.

Their mother, Mary, was pinning out wash when the boys walked slowly up, Goeff first, Gordie shuffling behind, so she knew something was amiss. Her elder son was strict about keeping the younger in tow, not allowing him to take the lead.

"What now? Come here and don't be hiding. Ah, what a mess you've made of yourselves! Take your hand from your mouth so I can see the damage. Do as I say! Oh! There'll need be doctoring for this. Your father won't be pleased. Nor will you when he finds out. The fighting may pass him by, but not the expense. Gordie, I can't keep this from the man."

"I know, Ma."

"Not your brother did this. Who?"

"Young Henry. He was fishing and we chunked some rocks at him."

"You what? Why on earth?" For Mary, life was trouble enough without creating more.

"I felt like it." Gordie was as honest as his brother was evasive.

"As blunt as that," sighed Mary sadly. "You'd be better off if you could learn to lie like Goeff. No doubt you'll make the same admission to your Da'?"

"I'm not afraid of telling the truth to him." And this was true.

"A little fear can save a lot of suffering," muttered Mary in response, then sighed again: "Well, done is done. Stay out of sight when he gets home and pray he's saved his drinking for tonight. I'll say I sent you to bed early from being sick of your shenanigans, which I am. Better wait until morning to confess about today. When he's rested and in a better temper. Even so, it will be hard with you. For now, we best be seeing Doc to get you sewn back up."

Boys! Twenty dollars that they didn't have to spend Mary spent to save her son a scar on his face. Boys! Why didn't God give her at least one girl? Better the expenses of dances and dresses than bandages and broken bones. But no. In His infinite wisdom, He had seen fit to bless her motherhood with sons. And what could she do but bear what she was given? No dreams to come true in this world. Maybe in the next.

First, to arise the next morning, Mary woke up her sons who had not slept well for worrying, imagining the worst. Then back to her bedroom to prepare MacGregor with the news, softening, she hoped, his reaction by sparing him a surprise.

"Whos' fun idea was this?" He looked from one boy to the other.

"Mine, Da'." Gordie stepped forward to assume full responsibility.

"And I'm to pay the doctoring, is that it? Is that what you expect?"

"I'll work it off," said Gordie evenly. Goeff spoke not a word.

"Oh will you?" mocked MacGregor with disdain. "And what work have you in mind? More to the point, have you in hand?"

"I'll find work," Gordie's sincerity cut through his father's scorn which both pleased and provoked MacGregor, wanting his son to stand up to him, resenting it when Gordie did, now directing his resentment to Goeff.

"And you, Goeff? You! Are you no better than a tag along? Have you no will of your own except to follow your brother?"

But Goeff was not to be drawn into argument.

"Whatever you say is what I am, Da'," the younger son replied. How could MacGregor argue with agreement?

"So that's half settled: I'm to be repaid. Now for the other half: punishment for making mischief with the summer folk." Here MacGregor unbuckled his belt and withdrew the leather strap from around his waist.

"Five licks for you Gordie, for starting the trouble. Three for you Goeff, for joining in. Who's first?"

Obediently Goeff turned around and leaned forward against the side of the house to receive his due. Worse than the pain was the anticipation. So it came as a relief when he felt the stinging blows – one, two, three – welting his skin and watering his eyes. Then it was over. His father was mercifully swift.

"Now you, Gordie. Come! I've more important work than your backside. Turn about!"

But Gordie did not move except to plant his feet and confront his father, hands clasped behind his back.

"Oh, so it's to be like that is it?" Among the tales of his coming up MacGregor had told the boys how, at about their age, he had resolved to take punishment from his father like a man, straight on with no complaint. What Gordie had decided to do now, his mouth drawn tight to suppress any expression of pain, eyes unflinching in the face of discipline to come.

MacGregor nodded stern approval of his son's decision, determined to honor Gordie with the cleanest blows he could deliver, laying the strap evenly across one leg and then back with equal force across the other. One, two, three, four, five. Not a grimace to be seen. Punishment was well delivered and well received.

The whipping over, the lesson remained to be given. MacGregor spoke to the point.

"You leave the summer folk alone. Particularly Young Henry. I need all my advantages to beat his father, and now you've gone and put me in the wrong. To make things right, I'll have to blame myself for this." Both boys felt their father's shame as well as guilt for causing it. The Trout King should have to apologize to no man, much less to one who sought the title for himself.

MacGregor shook his head in disgust.

"So that's done," he concluded, one task down and the rest of the day to go. Replacing his belt, then hoisting a sling of tools over his shoulder, he turned and walked away, calling back as he left, "And after you've scraped and sanded the metal chairs, you can prime them too," adding another task to one the boys already had been given. More work as penance for misconduct.

"So that's done," whispered Mary to herself, having witnessed her husband's rough justice from the porch, powerless to stop the severity of which she did not believe. Although the boys found her corrections worse, sermons to which they were obliged to listen. Sermons lasting longer than the sting of their father's belt. Which they had told her, while she disagreed: how could words of improvement hurt worse than the heavy hand of punishment?

After putting both boys to chores Mary set off on her two-mile walk to town, MacGregor having taken their only vehicle to make his rounds of summer houses, attending to whatever needed upkeep and repair. For whom he worked, exactly what he did, was mostly a mystery given the man did not confide his days to her at night. What she did know Mary inferred from parts of jobs he parceled out to Gordie and Goeff for learning skills they would have needed as men.

Nor did she bore or burden him with drab tales of her own daily doings. Conversation about each other's drudgery, where was the pleasure in that? Rather talk about the past or future than the present, good times remembered and better times to come. Important for them each to get away, he fishing in the early morning by himself or with the Reverend late afternoon, and come evening closing down the day with other Tavern regulars celebrating release from work. While time away she was service to the church and took Wednesdays, as her day for visiting with friends. Today.

As she slowly climbed the porch steps dragging her weariness behind her, Mr. Detmer stood up and smiled welcome, pulling open the door and announcing her arrival inside.

"Cora! It's Mary. Mary MacGregor come to see you!"

Years ago, having sensed that she was shy of men, Mr. Detmer had extended Mary the courtesy of not greeting her directly when they met, which she appreciated, not having to greet him back. Removed from the security of home and familiarity of family, she was ill at ease in public, prey to anxieties which years of following MacGregor from job to job, from place to place, had grown within her. Those were the years on the road when she had no companion save her husband, and not even him when he was off at work. Those were the years when she was all alone.

Until they came to Bishop's Place there was no opportunity for friends because until the boys she had no power to make MacGregor settle down. But motherhood, family, and home gave her a say she did not have before, inspired in her a fierceness he respected. While he began to earn their living she began to sink their roots, and in the process keep a promise to herself. This was the promise she had made for the sake of hope when hope was all that kept loneliness from wandering at bay. Bishop's Place was her chance, and she took it.

Mustering courage, Mary had gone in search of friends with absolutely no idea of how to find them. Self-effacing, she had none of her husband's boldness to command attention and provoke a response. And yet, Cora Detmer could tell from her hesitant but resolute approach how Mary was shopping for more than mere provisions that first day. In the strange woman's reticence, she sensed an invitation. So, engaging the newcomer at once in easy conversation, Cora pierced the veil of shyness and found sincerity she liked, a capacity for plain speech equal to her own, and a worldliness from travel she did not possess, having spent her entire life in Bishop's Place.

Mary was adopted on the spot. As a friend and something more, as a child. Since Cora had no sons or daughters of her own, she established maternal interest where she could, caretaking those she chose to care about. And she found Mary in dire want of caring when it came to the man, MacGregor. In a proper marriage, a man's place was underneath a woman's thumb. Like her father deferring to her mother. Like she and Wally, he content to do her bidding, she is willing to provide for his direction. So it was about home and marriage Cora usually inquired first.

"Mary! You've come. I suppose you've walked to town and not been driven?" Implying in the question of disapproval of how her friend was being treated.

"The walk is good for me, Cora. Besides, I like it. As for MacGregor, he was early off. It's his busy season, you know. And how are you?" Mary turned the question back to let Cora know she had not come to visit to discuss her husband's failings. Cora is giving in.

"I'm as good as a business, which is pretty brisk." Truly spoken. Summer trade gave her a blush of vitality that slow winter months soon paled away. Cora was at her best at her busiest.

"Wally! Bring us two sodas, cold, and mind the front with Mother. We'll be sitting out back for a while." Turning to her friend: "Now, Mary, tell me about the boys. What they've been up to?"

It was an invitation Mary welcomed and Cora was pleased to give – a chance to talk and hear about the trials of mothering, satisfying for each woman a need. For Cora, this was a chance to ask herself what she would do in Mary's stead because Mary would appeal to her as an authority on motherhood despite Cora's barren experience on the subject. Having only her own upbringing as a reference, Cora nonetheless did provide a source of fixed opinions upon which Mary could depend and derive a measure of support.

"Why, Cora, why would Gordie and Goeff go pick a fight for the fun of it? What fun?"

"The fun of doing what they know they shouldn't. Idleness, Mary. Free time is meant for mischief. Its work keeps youngsters out of trouble. Work and paying for what trouble they make." Cora believed in the religion of Industry which she had been indoctrinated early by a mother who taught by inexhaustible example.

"Punishment, you mean? Well, there's been that." And Mary described MacGregor's choice of consequences, an explanation that left Cora in the uncomfortable position of approving as father the man she disapproved as husband. So she changed the conversation.

"Can you believe it, Mary? The men are at it again. At Wally's contest. All for the sake of who can catch the biggest fish, as though it matters. All for the boasting rights if you ask me. Trout King, indeed! Who cares who owns the title? It brings little good but local glory. Makes me grateful I'm a woman, not having to compete in such nonsense." Then seeing Mary's face turn hurt, immediately mended what she had said: "No discredit to your husband, of course. Him winning the title each year. I know you must be proud."

Mary smiled at the grudging respect her friend felt called upon to give.

"No Cora, boasting rights mean self-respect when you're a man. Attention paid counts for a lot when there is little else to earn. MacGregor's earned his right to boast. Let him enjoy it. Remember, men are not like you and I, content with getting by. They want to make a mark to be remembered when they're gone." Having grown up with this sexual distinction in her own family, Mary had grown even more accustomed to it living with MacGregor.

"Nonsense!" Cora replied. "A living is mark enough to make. My Wally's never wanted more. Nor Father either. Except for Mother and myself minding the business, Detmer's Dry Goods and Groceries would have folded long ago. Keeping things going, that's women's work. And getting men they marry to follow after. As for your husband, Sam Henry, and the rest, if making something serious of play is what they want, why I suppose it's up to them. Being a man, I guess Wally knew they would."

Just then her husband's voice burst in upon them.

"Cora, come see! Sam Henry's here and by God this time I think he's caught a winner! Come inside!"

Both women immediately responded, Cora in spite of herself catching the contagion of excitement from Wally's voice. Gathering around, they joined Mr. Detmer who was looking unusually somber, staring at the swaying scale, while Sam was all smiles, eagerly awaiting official confirmation of how much his entry weighed, the largest trout he had ever caught.

"Almost five pounds! Wally, what do you think? Is that some fish? All I'm lacking is the look on MacGregor's face when he sees what he's got to beat." Then he noticed the new arrivals.

"Cora! Mrs. Mac, you too! Say, a while back your husband gave my son a message for me. Would you return the favor now? Thank Mac for saving the big brown for me in Grisham's Well. Tell him I'm much obliged. Knowing the river so well, no doubt he knew about it all the time." And Sam couldn't keep from laughing at his joke.

Mary nodded but said nothing back. She had never liked Sam Henry. Not just because he was her husband's closest fishing rival. She'd never liked his easy way with words or his perpetual good humor – both signs to her of someone who'd been born to luxuries her husband had to do without, MacGregor bound to work while Sam was free to play.

Now her aversion for him mixed with dread. Only once before had MacGregor caught a trout so large, many years ago, the first year he laid claim to being Trout King. By his own admission, he was unlikely to luck into one that size again. This meant he was about to forsake title, pride, and worse, what little cheerfulness long summer hours at work allowed him to bring home at night. Later at night, because he would stay later at the Tavern easing humiliation from his loss with drink.

"Well I best be going, Cora. I mustn't keep Ojay waiting when she's put lunch with me ahead of fishing."

Mary's second stop on her day in town: Ojay's Café and Tackle. Ojay her other female friend, a rough and tumble woman who had recognized in Mary a survivor like herself and had immediately like what she had seen.

Cora half listened to her friend's goodbye, the more attentive half preoccupied with business, selling refreshments to the gathering throng that word of mouth had now attracted off the street.

"Next week then, Mary. And if you think of it, tell Ojay her order's in."

But by then Mary was out of hearing, having fled the painful celebration taking place, having fled Cora's obtuseness to her pain. Ojay would understand.

And did. Sensing distress from Mary's hurried entrance through the door, Ojay quickly came round the counter and led Mary to a booth.

"There. No talk until you've rested." And Ojay hustled off quickly returning with a steeping cup of steaming tea that Mary slowly drank in silence, grateful for the consideration being shown. Then she recounted her experience at Detmer's, how it felt, how she had to leave.

Ojay nodded her head.

"Yes, that's Cora. A good friend but insensitive as a post. Her way the only way. Just like her mother. Both of them born 'right'. I never heard of either one changing their mind, much less admitting they was wrong. Once Cora fastens onto an opinion, she don't let it go. Don't make no difference I've been on my own since age fourteen, in Cora's mind I'm still as much in need of care as way back then. No, Mary, you ain't going to change her thinking. Not about fishing, fishing contests, or MacGregor. No matter he be reeling from the blow. This trout is bigger than the one he caught eight years ago."

"You've seen it then?" asked Mary.

"Yes. Sam stopped here first. We're friends that way. Fishing friends. He shows me what he catches if it's any good. Wants to convert me from bait to flies, while I keep nagging him to leave his religion for mine. Don't do either of us any good, but being fishermen we don't give up. No quitting sense. Showed me the nymph he tried to take the one today. A Pilot's Wife he called it. Looked like a tiny burr. Now how'd he catch something so big on something so darn small? He's all fisherman in his way Mary. The only real competition MacGregor's had." Then leaning forward she patted Mary's arm: "How's he doing with the news?" Meaning MacGregor.

Mary shook her head.

"Not well I'm sure when the news finds him out. Not well for the boys and me when he gets home. I've prayed and prayed for him to win easily so we don't suffer through another summer like the last, him behind and Sam Henry ahead. But this is worse. Tell me the truth, does MacGregor stand a chance?"

Ojay looked away in search of comfort and then looked back, evading what was asked with a question of her own.

"Winning the title means so much? To you, I mean. I know it does to Mac."

"But he won't win, will he?" asked Mary again. And then added reflectively, "It's hard to lose the one good thing in life that life has given. To have it stolen by another who already has so much. It's just not fair!"

Ojay had never heard Mary express animosity before.

"Luck's not fair, Mary. Luck is luck. MacGregor's had his run. Maybe it's Sam's turn now."

Mary's own voice grew soft but became ungentle. Not a whisper, but a hiss.

"Turn? Sam Henry deserves no turn! MacGregor has a right to the title. He belongs to the town and the title belongs to Bishop's Place. And you know it, or you should. Do you want some outsider taking it home to laugh about with his city friends? Laugh at us? Do you? The title belongs here because it's important here and nowhere else. And who's to thank for keeping it in town? MacGregor, that's who!"

Aroused by Mary's anger, Ojay awakened to a sense of threatened pride. The town was about to lose something important.

"Go on," she asked, in need of hearing more.

But Mary returned to her original question.

"So there is no chance for MacGregor?"

Ojay solemnly agreed.

"I've known about Sam Henry's fish for going on three years. In our part of the river, it's about as big as trout can grow."

Hearing the verdict she feared, Mary hung her head.

"So be it," she murmured. If anyone could rule on local possibilities it would be Ojay. She was the authority. Even

MacGregor admitted that. Inch by inch she'd fished the east branch of the river for more than thirty years. Mary slumped over in defeat.

"The largest fish but one," Ojay corrected.

"What?" Mary looked up. "But one? Do you know another? Where?"

Ojay smiled at the humor of it.

"Where Sam Henry would never think to try. At least not now. In Grisham's Well."

"No," contradicted Mary. "This trout he caught, it came from Grisham's Well. The biggest in the pool, he said."

Ojay agreed.

"He's almost right. But I know better 'cause I have seen them both. The one he caught and the one he didn't know he missed. Both lay beyond where I can dunk a worm. Beyond where I thought Sam could toss a fly. He must have stretched himself to reach the one he did. But he'd have to throw half again as far to even tempt the other, and I don't believe he can."

"What about MacGregor?" asked Mary. "He's taller and stronger."

Ojay realized how little Mary understood.

"It's timing and rhythm gives distance to a cast as much as power. I don't know anyone can float a line so far except maybe the Reverend on a good day, the wind behind him and the Lord willing. But he casts better than he catches, so even if he set the hook he'd never fight it in. Sam or MacGregor might, but not the Reverend. A longer line just gives the trout more chance to get off. Always keep a short line myself. That way I get in what I get on."

Mary had been listening attentively, searching for hope in the discouragement Ojay had given. Although she knew nothing about fishing herself, Mary had absolute faith in her husband's prowess at the sport.

"Suppose MacGregor got closer to the fish and didn't have to make so great a cast?"

Ojay didn't like hearing bad news, but the truth was too apparent to deny.

"The pool's the problem, Mary. You can't change the pool. Anyone who knows the river will vouch for what I say. Water's too deep to wade. Too clear to use a boat without spooking the fish. The woods grow to the bank so there ain't no room for casting from the shore. The only clear approach is from below. But tricky still because the pool runs dogleg upstream maybe eighty yards. Sam must have cast a third the length to take his trout. Not bad. But shy by forty feet of where the bigger one still lays. In a deep trough where the river turns. It don't travel much. Don't have to. Just waits for food to come its way. Getting bait to it, there's the problem."

"Why can't you throw it from above or let the current carry it down?" Now Mary tried her hand at a solution.

"No," Ojay objected. "Headwaters is too fast and deep to take a steady stand. The noise you'd make keeping your balance would scare the fish downstream. No. It must be done from below if it's to be done at all." Then Ojay became quiet and thoughtful. She had dismissed this challenge for herself when she had first observed both fish. But now, with Mary's prompting, she was reconsidering. So it was to herself she spoke, not to her friend.

"I know its habits and its tastes. The Reverend might cast the distance. MacGregor might bring it in. Not one of us could do it alone. But together? Who knows? We might."

'Might'. The word was all the encouragement Mary needed to sustain her fragile hope.

"Shall I tell the Reverend? I always stop by there on my way home. And MacGregor? Shall I tell him?"

"Yes. Tell them to meet me here at daybreak tomorrow. The three of us can go and reconnoiter at Grisham's Well. With luck, we'll get to see the big one feed."

Immediately Mary was off, thanking Ojay, in a hurry to enlist the Reverend in a holy war against Sam Henry, in a righteous war to save her husband's reputation and the town's good name.

CHAPTER SEVEN

THE CONSPIRACY BEGINS

The fish of his dreams! The big brown trout Sam's fantasy had long imagined was a reality at last. Finally! Hard to accept. Most of the afternoon he'd spent gazing at his frozen trophy through the frosted glass at Detmer's, accepting congratulations, enjoying admiration, answering questions, telling and retelling the story of its conquest, unable to take his eyes off the dead fish for very long because catching it was so unexpected. The experience still felt unreal.

What he had told MacGregor was true. Not skill, but Luck would decide between them. Luck first and last. When he had not been looking, She had looked his way. She had blessed his efforts neither in spite or in consequence of what he tried. Just because. What he believed and why he loved the sport. Fishing was not for trout. Sam Henry fished for Luck. In his heart of hearts he was a gambler, the river where he took his risks and tempted Fate for play.

Front listened enthralled, savoring each detail of the story his father had to tell. Sam, relived the experience that evening as he described it.

"I don't know what got into me. It must have been the day. A perfect day. No glare on the river. Only the slightest breeze against my back. And that long avenue of open water. I just couldn't resist. Decided it was time to take my measure. To see what line I could deliver with conditions at their best. I thought of the Reverend and his joy of casting and asked myself, why not? Just for once, forget the fish and concentrate on going through the motions with all the grace and sensitivity I could. The Reverend's right, 'the beauty of the sport is in the cast'. The dance, he calls it. And I'm right too, the trickery's in trying flies. And MacGregor's right, success is what you catch. And Ojay's right, fishing is love of being on the river."

"And I'm right," interrupted Front. "Fishing is always hoping for a bigger fish tomorrow."

"Yes, that too," agreed Sam. "But today it was the Reverend's joy I wanted. To feel his pleasure at the beauty, so I did. Gave myself over to the purity of casting. The simple back and forth and the subtlety of timing. Getting the rhythm exactly right. Stripping line with each wave of the rod, feeling the weight increase the more I threw. Each pass waiting for the fullness of the curl to break behind me before pulling it forward, waiting for the forward curl to break before pulling it back. At last building speed for the final toss, line sailing through the guides like silk, further than I'd ever thrown before. The spool wound almost down to empty. My God, I'll never cast this far again, I thought, and began to reel in when something stubborn on the other end objected. Something heavy, with enough authority to stop my line. I don't know what I thought it was, but not a strike. You see my mind was still caught up in casting. Mostly it felt like a tug of disagreement over just whose fly it was. Since it was mine, I tugged right back. Then the trout cleared up any confusion." He paused in wonder and then continued. "You know how no two fish will fight the same? Well, this one had a style of his own, unhurried as the current. That steady and that strong. He just leaned on his weight and began lazily swimming bank to bank. No sign of panic. He seemed to know I couldn't speed him up or slow him down. And no surprises. He didn't rush at me to loosen line and slip the hook. He didn't dive to wedge himself behind a rock. He didn't even bolt for daylight, head upstream. It made no sense. A whole half pool of freedom and he stays down at my end. What's keeping him penned in? Not me. So he just took his time and mine. Lap after lap. Maybe thinking I'd tire of holding on before he tired out. But I didn't. And he did. It took a while."

"How long?" asked Front.

"Thirty, maybe forty minutes. I've never had a fish play me that way before. Conserve his energy so carefully. I told you they were smart. He just hung in there til he had nothing left. Ran out of gas. Stalled in the water. Then I just reeled him in. He didn't even shy when he saw the net. That spent. What a sight! They're all so beautiful. The blood red-purple of the Brookie. The shining silver of the Rainbow. The golden yellow of the Brown. Heavy as gold was how he felt when I lifted him. A golden trophy. Yet there was something missing. He was big and beautiful all right. But I felt disappointed. For all the time it took to land him, my skill had not been tested. Patience was all it took to wear him down. Besides, I wasn't even casting for a fish. What I had told MacGregor, not skill but Luck would decide between us. Luck had simply looked my way."

While Front appreciated Sam's confession of humility, he wanted to attribute enough accomplishment to the father to make the son proud.

"But you tied the fly. You made the cast. You set the hook. You played him in. You could have lost him and you didn't."

Sam smiled. "You're right. I better take my credit where I can. Why Stel, even you were impressed."

It was true. While not a fishing enthusiast, Estelle was moved by her husband's achievement.

"You know what struck me, Sam? How excited people were down at the store. How much they seemed to care about who won. How much the contest matters. Not to you, I know. But to the people here. I was treated like the wife of a celebrity. Why Cora and her mother actually congratulated me!"

"Yes," Sam agreed. "You're right. Old Mr. Detmer tried to tell me so a while back. I kind of brushed him off. I wasn't meaning to be rude, but his dead seriousness was ruining my fun. After all, outside of Bishop's Place, who ever heard of the Trout King? Or cared?"

"Still," argued Front, "you will enjoy winning if you do."

"Are you trying to keep me honest?" Sam laughed. "Yes. Not taking the title so much as proving after all these years MacGregor can be beat. His boasts have a ring of truth I'm tired of hearing. No fun in losing. Now, what are we going to do about you?"

"What do you mean?" Front didn't understand.

"I've caught my big fish," Sam explained. "Now it's time to work on catching yours. How about joining me at the west branch tomorrow? A lot of state records have been pulled from the stream. Even more have been lost. Whoever designed it liked deep rips, lots of turbulence, and big boulders. You'll be doing more climbing than wading. And it's rainbows you'll be after, not browns. So you'll get your money's worth if you get anything. The current alone will double the fight of whatever you catch. But you'll have to fish wet. The water's too fast to float a fly. Are you willing?"

Front was delighted. The invitation meant his father now considered the boy's capacities up to the challenges posed by a larger and more difficult river.

As for Estelle, she was not so sure, although she kept her worry to herself. It was another tension in their marriage, how much risk from fishing should Front be allowed to take. Her instinctive caution against his love of adventure.

"Shall I bring anything special?" asked Front.

"Yes," answered Sam, meaning to assure Estelle by what he told his son. "More carefulness than usual. If you get one on and have to follow it downstream, remember no trout is worth breaking your neck over. I'll put you in above me so if you do fall in I can catch you from below. But don't feel you have to give me that chance. Rescuing a flailing son from foaming water can be tougher than landing a record fish."

Front smiled at the image, but understood the warning being given. And why. "I'll be careful," he promised both his parents.

"Then we're agreed," said Sam. "I'll wake you at about four o'clock and we'll stop on the way at Ojay's to get some breakfast. I called her and she'll be ready for us. Plenty of food for you and advice for me, unless I'm much mistaken. It's the old argument, artificial lures against live bait. My use of flies against her use of worms. We're both right and we each know it, but neither will admit that to the other. Truth is, she understands the river better than anyone. That's the reason why her store enjoys the trade it does. People who know enough to appreciate her savvy keep dropping by for a cup of coffee and supplies. So they pretend. Really they come for tips on catching trout and news about what's hatching on the water."

"Why does Ojay go telling what she knows to strangers?" asked Front. "How come she doesn't keep it secret. I would. Like Mr. MacGregor keeping his tricks to himself."

"Yes," agreed Sam. "But I think you'll find MacGregor is exception to the rule. Most fishermen are very generous about passing on discoveries. Maybe because they have a common adversary in the trout. Why I've given flies away to guys I didn't even know and never saw again. They weren't taking fish and I was so I'd share what was working for me. Other times I've had fishermen concede a pool they were about to try and when I finished casting my way up, we'd visit and exchange helpful ideas. It's an unpredictable way to get educated, but I've learned more from streamside acquaintances than from all the expert books I've read."

"I still wouldn't tell," argued Front, covering up what really was at issue, the feeling he knew nothing worth sharing. Wishing he did. Wishing he knew as much about fishing as his father.

"But if I ever do find something out important, I'll tell you."

"Thank you, Front," Sam valuing the promise.

That night the boy's dreams kept waking him up, waking him up early, restless with excitement, too excited to get back to sleep, eager for the day's adventure to begin. Out of bed the instant he heard Sam. By 4:15, they were on the road.

"This is kind of early for you and I, but it's regulation rising time for Ojay. She doesn't like the sun to beat her up. Fact is, if it wasn't for feeding us, she'd be hunkered down on some old rock by the river, still as a heron, taking whatever time it took to catch some poor benighted trout that caught her eye." Sam was talking himself awake. "Made the mistake one time of admiring her patience and she struck back quick as a snake 'Patient? I ain't patient! Never have been. But I'm bone stubborn, and the fish ain't been made can wear me down with waiting.' Which is probably true. Anyway, be sure to listen to what she has to say. You'll pick up a good idea or two. I always do. Although I'd never admit that to her."

They pulled off the highway at a dimly lit bungalow, on first inspection a residence, on second a restaurant, on third both. Through the plate glass window, they could see a figure hunched over the counter staring out. The sign on the front door read: IF I'M FISHING, I AIN'T OPEN. IF I'M OPEN, I AIN'T FISHING.

"Morning gents. What'll it be?" The question was a matter of form since Ojay served one standard breakfast, the only choice being to subtract unwanted items from the full order.

"I'll have the works," answered Front with the air of an old customer, which in fact he was.

"Coming up. How about you, Mister?" Part of the charade was treating Sam initially as though he was a stranger.

"Hold the potatoes and sausage, and I'll have coffee, black, thank you." Sam acted out his part impersonally in response.

Ojay turned to the grill and soon the crackling and spattering of frying were entertaining their senses. Still facing away from them she tossed a question over her shoulder.

"Taking the boy to new fishing grounds?"

Sam smiled as the banter between them began.

"To the west branch. Bigger waters, bigger fish they say. I've caught mine. Thought I'd give Front here a chance to catch his."

Ojay sniffed as though she smelled an insult.

"Bigger water, maybe. That's all. Our fork of the river can equal any trout you're likely to catch over there, and then some. Ain't no geographic cures for what ails you, including bad fishing. Besides, no point trekking off for what you got as good or better close by." Protective of the river's reputation she took a proprietary stand on its defense.

"Now Ojay, you know we're not putting down the east branch of the river by fishing the west one."

"Not saying you are," Ojay retorted. "Only testifying to what I know. Closing in on forty years fishing this branch and I've caught my share of trout, in season and out, not traveling much beyond my own back door."

"No argument there," Sam replied.

And Front relaxed as the friendly opposition between the two fishermen began to build, so different from the painful bickering between his parents.

"Here's your drinks," Ojay turned away, quickly turning back. "And here's your eats," a heaping plate for Front and a full one for his father.

"Suppose you're fixing to use flies?" Ojay innocently asked.

"Suppose so," Sam replied as though this was the first time she had ever broached the subject.

"Well of course that's up to you," Ojay consented. "Ain't my place to question what you teach your son."

"I'm sure you wouldn't," laughed Sam, "but I'm sure you will."

And they were off like a couple of seasoned performers dancing through a well-rehearsed routine.

"I'm only pointing out," Ojay continued, "the advantages of natural bait over the artificial item. Feeding fish live food is easier than fooling them with fakes."

"True enough," Sam conceded. "But imitation adds to the challenge."

"Not for me," Ojay objected. "Why take something as God given plain as slipping a worm on a hook and fancy the sport up with a lot of thread and feathers when results ain't no better and often ain't as good? Why you're going to educate the common sense out of the boy. Show him how to keep it simple and you'll be doing him a favor."

Sam shook his head.

"Ojay, you leave out half the fun. The craft of tying flies and the elegance of casting. The subterfuge of using make-believe."

"Now listen, Sam, which are you after, catching fish or creating difficulty?"

"Both," Sam admitted.

So back and forth they parried, neither one seriously wounding the other's arguments, each enjoying the abiding difference between them.

"Here," Ojay shifted the conversation at last. "What do you suppose this is good for?" Something clanked on the counter. It was a hinged metal ring such as Front used at school to bind his work together. The kind you could pull open, insert through punched holes in paper, then snap shut again.

"Let me guess," offered Sam. "You dangle it above the water to tempt any trout in the market for a wedding ring. Then, when window shopping attracts them to the surface for a closer look, you net them without having to bait a hook. Am I close?"

"Very perceptive," Ojay smiled. "As usual, I can't praise your intelligence too highly. For your information this ain't no attraction at all. It's an irritation. A genuine, bona fide fish irritator. In the unlikely event you ever become stuck to a big fish in deep water what refuses to budge, this little gadget can help. It saved me last week. I was in a boat plumbing for lake trout with tackle too light for the job and this item worked like a charm. Had a big one on, but couldn't bring him up. He just lay there waiting for me to come down. So I put this ring around my line and let gravity take it to the fish. Couldn't move him before, but as soon as this bumped against his nose he was off the bottom and up in a fighting hurry." She tossed it to Sam. "Hold onto it. Maybe if nothing else, it will change your luck one of these days when your luck needs turning."

Sam slipped the ring into one of his vest pockets.

"Thanks Ojay. Like you say, in this uncertain business you never know what's going to come in handy." Then he excused himself, stood up and walked to the rest room.

"Son, come here," Ojay called to Front from the far end of the counter. "I want to show you something. Your father knows his flies, I'll give him that. No two better fishermen than him and MacGregor, but don't you say I said so or I'll never hear the end of it. But he don't know it all. There's a few tricks he could steal from bait fishing if his mind wasn't so closed to the subject. Course I'm not proposing you go against your Dad's instruction. That's his right. You're his boy and imitation is his way."

Then she rummaged under the counter and came up with five round lead pellets, each half cut open, which she placed before Front.

"Sam's going to have you casting streamers if I know him. They may do just fine. Or they may not. If the day wears on and you haven't hooked anything, you might try this. Take two or three of these split shot and pinch them to your leader about twelve to fifteen inches due north of the fly. To attach them put the nylon in the crack and bite down with your teeth til the lead squeezes shut. Got the idea so far?"

Front nodded.

"Good," Ojay continued. "Then find you a comfortable rock about a third of the way out that you can safely reach, where the water's running deep and long on the down river side. Climb out and toss your line into the current until the sinkers catch bottom. Hold it right there. Reel in the slack. Now what's going on which you can't see is that streamer waving back and forth down deep just like a minnow still-fished on a hook. You let it be. It's anchored so it ain't going anywhere. Problem with most fly fishermen is they're in too much of a hurry to stay put. You just sit back and wait. Nothing small will smack your fly fishing this way, but something big just might. Now quick, here comes your Dad. Stuff these in your pocket and not a word!"

With her other hand Ojay picked up a rag and began to mop the surface of the counter.

"Talking with your boy here," as though she had been discussing nothing of consequence, "has given me some hope for him yet. In spite of how you've taught him, he might just catch something today." Then looking at Front, "Let me know if you do any good."

"I will, Ojay. Thanks. Thanks for the breakfast I mean." What Front like best about Ojay. Unlike other adults in his world she treated him grown up, as a fellow fisherman, no less.

"You're going to let us leave without advice?" asked Sam after paying.

"Advice?" protested Ojay. "Now what would a simple hook and liner like myself have to offer fishermen who fancy cast with flies?"

This uncharacteristic confession of humility caught Sam's attention. However, he was eager to get going and so shrugged the comment off. On their way out they were surprised by MacGregor and the Reverend coming in.

MacGregor spoke first to get it over with. Worse than congratulating a better was admitting to a wrong.

"You've minnowed my four pounder with your brown, Sam. And put a fair distance between us in the bargain. As for your message to Mary, you're welcome to the fish, but not the title. Not yet."

Sam laughed.

"You're in this with me to the bitter end, eh Mac? Good. Where there's time there's hope. And who knows, I might just catch one bigger." Sam meant this as a joke.

"If there's bigger fish to be caught, I'll do the catching," MacGregor as serious as Sam was amused. Then the burly man abruptly turned on Front.

"About that ruckus at the river. I'm sorry. If my boys didn't know better before, they do now. They won't spoil your fishing again."

Front was not expecting an apology.

"Thank you," he stammered. "Thank you for taking care of it. I hope Gordie's mouth is OK."

But MacGregor, having discharged his obligation was not inclined to carry conversation any further. He had withdrawn into disinterest, so Sam took advantage of the silence to greet the other man.

"I don't know, Reverend," Sam began. "You may be damaging your reputation by the company you keep. Meeting at odd hours in out of the way places with fishermen of all people -- known for stretching the truth when it's good and lying when it's bad. And you a man of the cloth!"

The Reverend responded to this banter in kind.

"Now what kind of minister would I be, Sam, if I shied away from sin? Or didn't sin occasionally myself, as MacGregor here will swear. Fishing a sin we both commit together, keeping each other as honest as we can, right Mac?"

"Time's a wasting," muttered MacGregor. "And this time of year that's sin enough. I've work to do."

"And we need to hit the road," replied Sam, feeling Front's impatience to get started. "Talking about fishing won't catch trout."

"But then again it might," interrupted Ojay who now joined them. "There's talk and there's talk. Good luck to the two of you!"

And Sam left feeling something was afoot, although he could not imagine what.

"You shouldn't even give the man a hint," growled MacGregor. "He's not in need of more advantage than he has."

"You're wrong there, Mac," Ojay objected. "It's no advantage to wonder if there's something up. It's a distraction. How can he concentrate on fishing when his mind is nagging him with doubt? No, you let me handle Sam Henry."

"Now what's this all about?" demanded the Reverend as the three sat down for coffee. "Yesterday Mary rushes in all astir about my being here today. Something about a bigger fish than Sam's. Something about saving the reputation of the town. Confused she was. Excited. Not making sense. If I didn't know better, I might have thought she was the one who drank too much and not MacGregor here."

Ojay declined to step into the breach. She knew their friendship encompassed many conflicts, this being one.

"Bah!" swore MacGregor. "Leave the drinking alone. If I haven't put up the bottle for Mary am I likely to put it up for you?"

"No. And there's the pity for your family," countered the Reverend sternly, no more inclined to quit taking his friend to task than MacGregor was to be taken without striking back.

"Don't be playing holier than thou with me, Reverend, or else I'll preach it back to you. You who've none to care for but yourself and stoop to live off Sunday offerings from others. Get you a family to support and an honest trade, and then we'll see if you're the man you say the rest of us should be. As for after work, show me man who don't take a dram when day is done and I'll show you a man who's not a man!"

"Meaning me?" the Reverend knew he did. One reason why he liked MacGregor. The man had absolutely no respect for his position. He could be freely spoken with MacGregor because his friend had no restraint with him. No one else in Bishop's Place talked to the Reverend in such irreverent terms, terms that even Ojay found offensive, and she no more a churchgoer than MacGregor who left attending Sunday services to Mary and the boys.

"Easy Mac," she said to calm his ire, "and you too Reverend." Warning the other man away. "I didn't bring you here to start an argument. Did Mary tell you what I told her?" This addressed to MacGregor.

The big man nodded.

"She did. I know the spot you mean. But I can't reach it."

"No you can't," she agreed. "But unless you do Sam Henry leaves this summer taking the title with him. And Sam Henry's gain is the town's loss. How would that suit you, Reverend?"

"Why it would suit me fine," the Reverend sharply replied. "The title has become a cursed vanity. One more false idol to distract us from what truly matters. Good riddance, I say. Who needs it?"

"Oh God! Will you listen to the man?" exclaimed MacGregor with disgust. "Who needs it? I do, Reverend. That's who. You can wait for glory in the hereafter. Me, I'll take mine here!"

"It's like this, Reverend," Ojay cut in, "About forty feet above where Sam caught his big brown there lays a larger one in deeper water. Ruler of the pool and a choosy eater. I know, I've watched it feed. No artificial lures accepted. Only the real thing will do. One hundred and twenty feet of line to reach from fisherman to fish, and the bait must land alive and kicking exactly over where the lunker lays. Could you do it, Reverend?" Would you if you could?"

The Reverend leaned back to consider this proposal. Ojay was not asking the right question. Should he do it? Should he seriously commit to a worldly competition when he was supposed to be above the fray? Should he refuse and let Ojay, Mary, and MacGregor down? And the town? He looked across the table at the two looking expectantly at him. Neither were members of his congregation. Yet over the years he had become a member of theirs. The daily visits to Ojay's for a cup of coffee and a bit of fishing news. Meeting with MacGregor in late afternoons to catch and match the evening rise. Were these not rituals that mattered, acts of communion that affirmed a common faith? He could not argue with the metaphor he was creating, giving a heavy sigh that Ojay recognized as giving in.

"I knew we could count on you, Reverend!"

MacGregor reached across and clapped him on the shoulder:

"You didn't disappoint me, Reverend, and you won't be sorry. Now, can you make the cast?"

"I don't know," the Reverend replied, beginning to deliberate the task at hand. "I've never thrown so far. Perhaps. Double hauling with a weight forward line. Tournament style, someone beside me to hold the coils, to feed me line. Keep me free from tangles. I might. But live bait? We're talking six maybe eight false casts for distance before the final presentation. Maybe more. Whatever I was using would have to be well hooked or get torn off in flight. Even if it didn't die in travel it would be done in when it hit the water. Better an artificial fly."

"No," Ojay insisted firmly. "I know the fish. I know its likes. In a week or two the fields will give us what we need. They're starting to jump already, the big green and yellow grasshoppers. It's one of them   and   nothing   else."

The Reverend shook his head.

"The hook will kill the insect before the second cast."

"Then we won't hook it," said Ojay obstinately defending her choice.

This was too much for MacGregor.

"Do you mean to train it to hold on?"

Ojay ignored his sarcasm.

"I mean to figure out a way. And if I can't, I'll find someone who can. Sam Henry."

"Are you daft?" asked MacGregor in amazement. "Do you think the man's so full of charity he'd help his competition? Sam Henry doesn't care about the fish he catches. He doesn't even care about the title. It's beating me. That's the prize he's after."

"You're right," Ojay agreed. "He won't help you. But he just might help me, not knowing you and I and the Reverend were in cahoots. No, you just keep your fingers crossed and hope, pray if you like" (this to the Reverend) "that his son has a bit of Ojay's luck upon the river today."

Both men looked at her not understanding, while she made no effort to explain.

"So I'll give you an extra hand in casting, Reverend. We better do some practicing to get it right. When you've made the cast you pass the rod off to MacGregor. Of the three of us, he's best equipped to play so large a fish on so much line."

The Reverend nodded. It was true. The assignments were correct. He to reach the fish. MacGregor to fight it in. And Ojay to finagle how to hook a live grasshopper for long distance casting without doing it deadly harm.

CHAPTER EIGHT

OJAY'S LUCK

Back in the car, Sam was silent while they drove, thinking about something, the boy could tell. In no hurry to be told, Front searched the passing darkness for silhouettes of deer beside the road, occasionally catching the glow of headlights in their startled eyes.

"Now what do you suppose those three conspirators are up to?" Sam spoke at last.

"What do you mean?" Front suspected nothing.

"No," Sam continued his internal dialogue out loud. "The three best fishermen in Bishop's Place don't meet this early unless they've got some secret to discuss. But what?"

Front was in no mood to wonder about other people. He was wondering about himself. Wondering about the day. Wondering what luck might bring. Wondering if wanting luck got in the way of getting luck, feeling superstitious. His father, after all, caught his big trout when he had not expected to catch anything. Maybe Front should do the same, give up hope.

Impossible. His only way to give up hope was to hope giving up would do him good. Besides, without pleasure of anticipation he would sacrifice fishing's better half. The fun was in the wondering, was in the eagerness that tempted him from one cast to the next, the eagerness that made him restless now. Ready to reach the river, he was impatient to begin.

"Are we almost there?"

Letting go curiosity about the gathering at Ojay's, Sam turned attention to his son.

"Getting close," he answered. "I know how you feel. Still get as excited before a day's fishing as when I was your age. If fishing keeps a man young, this is how it's done – by renewing him with endless possibilities and dreams. Where would we be without dreams?"

"I'm dreaming of catching a big rainbow. Do you think I might?"

"Why not?" answered Sam, giving hope to the question Front hardly dared to ask. "A lot of big rainbows in the west branch and you've got as good a chance of tying into one as anybody else. One of the few good things you can say about Luck, she doesn't play favorites, but she's in on every play."

"I don't believe in luck that much," replied Front not wanting to. "I believe in keeping at it."

"Well, you're right there," Sam agreed. "Persistence counts for a lot in this business. The folks who catch the most are those who keep at it. Now, while we're driving, unsnap that silver tackle box hanging off my side and pick out what you want to start with. It's getting light enough for you to see."

Opening the lid the boy stared at row upon row of multicolored flies with small heads and long streamlined bodies, some of bucktail, some of feathers, some of both. Some on hooks so small he couldn't understand how his father's stubby fingers could be so precise. Some so large they looked like they would frighten fish more than attract them.

"What about this yellow and brown one with the little bit of white down its back?"

"The Yellow Daphne?" Sam looked over then back to keep his eyes on the road. "Good choice. I've used it with some success over here. You might want to take it up one size. Larger flies are heavier to cast but they seem to do better in a stream this rough. See what I mean?"

The car pulled off onto the shoulder of the road and parked. Looking down the steep embankment the boy saw a river twice as wide and turbulent as he was used to fishing, reminding him of the warning from the night before.

"I'll be careful," Front repeated his vow. "Do we get out here?"

"Yes," Sam pointed to a spot upriver from where they sat. "We'll put you in where those big rocks jetty out into the main current. Plenty of room for casting. Fish down from there. Take your time. I'll go in fifty yards below. If you get into something give a yell. I'll come up and net it for you."

By mid day Front had no cause to call for Sam's assistance. Neither father nor son had much on for very long. Front had briefly hooked a couple of small fish that had tugged themselves free, in one cast parting the leader and escaping with the fly. Holding too tight the boy had given the fish power to break him off, a lesson he would remember. Once he watched while his father bent into something that proved too strong to hold.

"Well they're in there and they're interested," observed Sam as they met. "At least we've made contact. Just goes to show how hooking a trout is no guarantee of catching it, even though I can't convince your mother of that uncertainty. One step at a time only gets you one step. Beats no strikes at all, but it's a long way from putting food on the table, which is not a bad idea. Why not give them a rest and have some lunch ourselves? We can change our flies to suit the afternoon. Different light favors different colors, although I don't know why. Hard to separate the superstition from the sense in this business."

Stretching out on a slab of stone half buried in the bank, they unpacked sandwiches, savoring the added flavor that eating in the outdoors gave. Sunlight shining down reflecting off the sparkling water relaxed both man and boy into a deep content.

"What kind of sense do you suppose trout have?" Front wanted to know.

Sam smiled.

"More than a lot of fishermen, many people would say. And they're probably right. Personally I don't think trout go in much for detail. They seem more sensitive to shape and outline, to shades of light and shadow, the kinds of subtleties we miss. Of course their hearing is much sharper than ours, at least underwater where it counts, while their reactions are infinitely quicker because like all wild things they live moment to moment. No past or future to distract them from the present. Then they respond to water pressure in ways we can't understand. As for smell, hard to say. Some bait fishermen swear odor matters. Maybe. Ojay could probably give you an informed opinion. But for survival, it's their instinctive sense of caution that keeps them alive. Unlike human beings, they have no need to act brave in the face of danger. Fear is their protector. And the bigger they grow, the more fugitive they become. Just the opposite of people."

Front started up from where he lay.

"Did you see that?"

"What was it?" Now Sam was sitting too.

"I don't know. All I saw was the hole that exploded in the water. Something big."

"Sounds like our signal,' said Sam climbing to his feet. "Let's get after them. We'll walk down a piece and I'll show you a good place to put in."

It was a promising spot that his father had found, a procession of low rocks, a few slightly submerged, leading like stepping stones out into the center of the stream to a flat, elongated boulder around which the river was forced to divide.

"Last year I hung into a really good one from here but the combination of his size and the rapids at his back was too much for me," confided Sam. "You'd think I'd know enough not to fight the current after all these years, but I didn't and the river won. All I can say is never underestimate the force of running water. Somehow, I still do. That's fishing, failure is more instructive than success. I tell you this so maybe you can learn from my mistakes. Good luck!" And Sam continued hiking down the shore.

Holding the fishing rod across his body like a tight rope walker keeping balance with a pole, Front carefully leapt from stone to stone until he landed on the long flat rock to which they led. An ideal location! Spread out before him was the entire width of the river within easy casting distance of both banks. No need to hurry. Carefully he assessed the surrounding water for telltale swirls and riffles that might hold a hiding place for trout. Slowly he tried them all, but to no avail. So he changed flies and tried them once again. Still no response. Frustrating. Maybe he should move on, and was about to when he remembered the advice that came with breakfast.

Well, why not? It wasn't how he'd been taught to fish, but then again it wasn't anything his father wouldn't try. So, pulling a couple of split shots from his pocket, Front attached them to the leader as instructed. Then he dropped the fly into the water and let the current carry it away. After feeling the sinkers hit bottom he reeled in the slack and sat back on his heels to wait. He wasn't used to waiting. He was used to moving while he fished, wading, and casting. Sitting still felt uncomfortable. What could he do while he was doing nothing? Searching around for something, he looked upriver then down, and saw his father waist-deep in foaming water, laying out those long easy casts the boy so admired. In hopes example would instruct, he studied the man's technique.

Warmed by the sun, cooled by the breeze, lulled by the sound of rushing water, preoccupied with watching Sam, Front began to lose track of time, of what he was doing. Having loosened his grip, he almost lost his pole as without warning it jerked free of his inattentive hand only to be recovered by reflexively throwing himself forward at the last moment to recapture his escaping gear. But not the line, which now sped from his reel in full pursuit of whatever was dashing off with his fly.

"YOWEE!" Front yelled to himself and to his father who, hearing his son's battle cry, glanced up, took in what was happening, yelled something back that Front could not understand, and stumbled frantically for shore.

His father's excited behavior brought Front to his senses. He couldn't catch this fish letting it go. Already a third of his line had been taken. Grasping the handle of the reel he gradually slowed the spin, curbing the trout's determined flight, causing it to turn to different tactics. Into the air the rainbow leaped, head shaking, body twisting, shedding a spray of water, trying to rid the pull from its jaw, flying fully extended over the river before it crashed back through the surface. Front gasped. Eighteen, maybe twenty inches! Down into the depth it dove, then up again, three, four times, each leap more acrobatic than the last. Each time Front prayed the fly would not be thrown. Each time his prayers were granted, the hook held fast. Now the jumps became less spectacular but still determined, the fish thrusting its body half out of the water, bending from side to side, sinking, thrusting up again, at last sinking for good, seeking refuge in deeper water where it began to dog, too tired to jump or run, but not to stubbornly resist. Planting his feet Front raised the rod high overhead to let the split bamboo wear down what strength remained, answering each exhausted tug with an untiring bend as the trout grudgingly yielded line.

"That's it!" shouted Sam from the bank. "Looks like he's getting winded. Can you make it over here without falling in? I can come to you."

Front shook his head.

"I want to move him from the middle. It will be easier." And very carefully he retraced his way across the stepping stones leaning against the fish's pull to keep his balance, standing at last beside his father who was out of breath from scrambling upriver, ready to help, net in hand.

"Okay!" encouraged Sam. "He's got a few bursts left. The sight of you and me should revive him some."

Front gave the trout a little line as it fulfilled his father's prediction, dodging warily away as it reluctantly approached its captors, weakly relenting allowing Front to slowly bring it in.

"That's a rainbow for you!" exclaimed Sam. "What a show! I've never seen so many acrobatics from a single trout. What a beautiful fish! You really got a good one this time. Okay. Keep easing him in.

Gentle, gentle. Now let me sneak below him with the net. Tail first so we don't warn him til he's caught. Keep reeling. Slowly now. That's it. A few more inches. Now!"

Sam took a swipe at the trout that must have sensed the net sweeping up from behind and turned at the last moment, bouncing off the metal rim, becoming reinvigorated by the contact, lunging away.

"Sweet Lord! I've lost him for you!" It was as close to despair as a non-despairing man could get. Sick was how Sam felt.

"No," Front corrected, his eyes riveted on the fish still bending the rod with its passive weight. "I've got him on. Try again."

"What a mercy!" Sam brightened up. "A second chance for stupidity. I won't miss him this time. Bring him round again and hold him steady in the current. Just like that. Now, over his tail and – WHOOPEE! You got him! In spite of my help. Great glory! You finally caught one to remember. Twenty inches is easy. What a fish!"

Squeezing the net shut above the gasping trout to prevent any accidents, Sam waded ashore and climbed halfway up the bank before feeling safe from further misadventure. Front followed along behind, connected to his father through the fishing line, stunned into silence, unable to believe what had occurred.

Together they sat down, the net resting on the ground between them. Curled around in a glistening silver circle, nose to tail in the confines of the mesh, lay the exhausted trout, natural brilliance fading as life began to ebb away.

Reaching into the net, Sam gripped the creature's broad neck with one hand. Seating the heel of his other hand on its head, he curled two fingers down over the mouth and hooked them underneath the lower jaw. Then, with a quick upward bend of his wrist, Sam snapped the trout's neck.

Front understood. Better for the trout to be killed quickly than to die slowly. But he still felt a mix of triumph and regret and said so.

"I'm glad I caught it, but part of me wishes I hadn't."

"Yes," Sam understood. "Quite a responsibility, gaming at the expense of a fellow creature's life. That's why your mother disapproves of the sport. It's not the same as fishing out of need."

No, it wasn't. But this had never troubled Front before.

"Why now?" the boy asked. "Why is this bothering me now?"

His father glanced at him and then at the trout as if in explanation.

"Catching your first big fish can change how you feel about fishing," the man replied. "Smaller trout seem less significant. They beg the question you are asking now. Is the trophy worth the cost? Should we kill for fun?"

Trophy! It was a trophy all right. Front felt a rush of pride overcome his ambivalence. And something else, the awakening of a possibility.

"I guess if I can catch one this size, I could catch one even bigger."

Sam smiled as he recognized where the boy's speculation was leading.

"I guess you could. Another change this fish creates. Raise your expectations. Opens the door. Before today you thought trout like this only happened to real fishermen. Now you've discovered you're as real as the rest of us. Now you're free to dare any ambition you want."

How did his father know? Front admitted what he had been thinking.

"Why I could even be the Trout King, couldn't I? Even beat Mr. MacGregor!"

"Yes," Sam laughed. "Welcome to the competition. Now that you've qualified, you've got as clear a shot at winning as anybody else. Welcome to the brotherhood of fishermen," and he gave his son a congratulatory hug. Then, Sam noticed something he had overlooked.

"What's this?" the man asked, observing a split shot on the leader. Curiously he looked at Front and then a thought occurred to him. Sam burst out laughing.

"There's the hand of a woman in this unless I'm much mistaken. And I don't mean your mother." Sam laughed some more. "Now what did that sly old fox tip you off to? I told you, she's as crafty as they come."

As though he was owning up to a guilty secret, Front disclosed the strategy he had been given.

"She told me to still-fish my fly. To anchor the line and let the current give it action. Then she told me to be patient, wait, and not be in a hurry to move on."

Sam was delighted.

"There's another page to take from her book. Never fished a streamer that way in my life."

"She told me to let her know if I did any good," Front said. "Can we stop off there on the way back?"

"We'll be sure to. Matter of fact we ought to head home pretty soon. You about ready?"

"Yeah. What a day!" answered the boy. "I'm ready."

But when they reached Ojay's, the restaurant was closed, the same sign offering the same explanation. IF I'M FISHING I AIN'T OPEN. IF I'M OPEN I AIN'T FISHING.

Front wrote a two-word message on a piece of paper and slipped it under the door: "It worked." To which Sam added a second message of his own: "P.S. I owe you one. Thanks."

CHAPTER NINE

THREE FISHERMEN AGAINST ONE FISH

"So your boy caught himself a good fish did he?" asked Ojay later in the week when Sam stopped by to pass the time of day.

"He did," Sam smiled with pleasure. "Thanks to you. Now he's ready for bigger and better luck to come."

"Well at least he's got the right attitude," laughed Ojay. "Poor old Luck! She can't never do enough. No sooner she gives us what we want than we want more. Fishermen is an ungrateful lot. Never satisfied for long."

"Yes," Sam agreed. "It would take catching a monster trout to kill a fisherman's ambition."

He sat down at the counter and stirred his coffee.

"Say," asked Ojay, as though the thought had just occurred to her. "Here's a problem for you, Sam. Grasshopper season is about to begin and I want to fish them different this year. Instead of dropping the little buggers hooked and half dead into the current, I want to throw them for distance and have them land no worse for wear than they was making the flight on their own. That lively. Any idea how to get this done?"

What Sam liked about Ojay, like himself she was always fishing for invention. Continuing to stir the spoon inside his mug he turned the question over in his mind.

"Not offhand," he answered at last. "Don't tell me you're taking up casting in your old age?"

"No. Just looking for variety is all."

"Yes. No way to have too much variety. Now let me get this straight. You want the grasshopper attached firmly enough for the flight in, but gently enough to land unharmed?"

"Can it be done?"

Sam welcomed the opportunity to return a favor.

"Give me a week or so. If you don't want the insect injured then you don't want it hooked. Which means devising some kind of cradle or harness on top of the hook. That's theory. Whether this would work in practice is something else. I'm going to have to think it through then try it out. Figuring is like fishing, you know. Takes a lot of tries to get what you're after. Even then, no guarantees. Got to be patient."

"No hurry." Ojay was glad to see her friend accept the challenge, pushing his change back across the counter, refusing payment for the drink.

"On the house," she announced. "I'll write it off. Cost of doing business. Ain't that the way you slickers do it in the city?"

Sam grinned. If it wasn't one difference between them it was another. He chided her in return.

"You give me too much credit Ojay, and you know it. Since when has city slick been any match for country sly?" Then he stood up to leave.

Looking hard at Sam to detect if he had spoken with suspicion, Ojay saw that he had not. Relieved she hadn't tipped her hand, she dismissed his question with a wave goodbye.

"And don't forget," she called after him, "the little critters need to fly first class all the way. A smooth ride and a three point landing."

"I'll remember!" Sam called back as he climbed into his car. Eager to get started, he drove down the highway in search of a place to begin. At last, rounding a curve, he found what he was seeking, an unmowed field of hay. Pulling alongside, he got out and waded through the tall grass kicking up grasshoppers with every step, easily capturing what he needed among such profusion, confining them to a lidded plastic cup for transport home.

At supper that evening he described his commission to Front.

"Is there a way I can help?" the boy asked, wanting to contribute if he could.

"Sure. Two of us are bound to be smarter than one of us. You can begin by keeping us supplied with grasshoppers. I have a feeling we're in for a lot of trial and error before we find what works."

As suspicious in her way as Sam was trusting in his, Estelle felt troubled by the repayment he was making and said so.

"Aren't you afraid of giving aide to the enemy? Suppose Ojay becomes Trout King with your help?" Not that she cared, except to her surprise Estelle found she did. Some part of her was tired of his losing too. Or at least, she enjoyed the notice winning gave.

"Ojay the enemy? No. You don't know the woman, Stel. It would take some powerful persuasion for Ojay to spoil her love of fishing for the sake of competition. Besides all these years she's shared ideas with me. Why, I'm just glad to give her something back."

Estelle was at an impasse and she knew it. Frustrating. What her pessimism sensed his optimism stubbornly denied. While Front, to relieve the tension between his parents did his part. He changed the subject.

"What do we do first?" he asked his father.

"The dishes," Sam replied, grateful for the diversion. "Then to the drawing board."

And so began the first of many evenings to follow when Sam, with Front's assistance and advice, attached all manner of tiny frames and saddles, cradles and contraptions, to bare hooks, fitting live grasshoppers onto the carriers, experimenting with different slips and loops and knots and ties to fasten the passenger down without damaging its body or restricting its wings. Then, next day, Sam would cast out creations from the night before only to see the grasshopper thrown off in flight, injured in transit, drown under the weight of heavy rigging, or partially escape captivity and splash into the water, insect facing one direction, hook and harness in another.

Discouraging. At least Front found it so, and shared what he was feeling with his father.

"Maybe it can't be done, what Ojay wants."

"Of course it can," Sam disagreed. "And we're on the way to finding how. Just look at the progress we've already made.

"I don't see any progress," argued Front. "So far we've nothing to show for our time but failure."

"That's right. A whole string of failures and a good thing too. Invention is a process of elimination, you know. That's where failure comes in. By demonstrating what doesn't work, it suggests what might."

Front had never thought of failure this way, as something to learn from. When he did, he felt better for their efforts. What his father said was true. They knew more now than they did at the beginning. And Front began to share the man's confidence, appreciating how experience one day shaped experiment the next, the device gradually becoming more workable until on the eighth day both could see they were getting close to a solution. Three of the first ten casts delivered the grasshopper as ordered. Alighting on the surface, each immediately tried to fly. However, on subsequent trials success fell to only four in twenty-five.

"Not good enough," Sam declared. "Ojay deserves better odds than that. But it sure is hard to figure where to simplify. Whipping against the frame is what's doing them in. But without the frame we lose the grasshoppers. Tie them down any tighter and we crush their insides. I can't think what else to change."

Front couldn't either. So he reviewed every strategy they tried. Then one more occurred to him that they had not -- the hook.

"If we could bend the hook a little, just enough to fit the body, maybe we could do without one of the forward holds."

"Maybe so," considered Sam, giving full weight to his son's suggestion. "You know, you may be right. We'll make some up tonight to throw tomorrow."

Next day, to their satisfaction, practice proved the problem solved. Not perfect, but reliable enough to present to Ojay in response to her request.

"You found the final piece to the puzzle," said Sam, "so you get to explain how it works. We can even collect some grasshoppers for her on the way over."

Ojay had been expecting Sam but not his son. So when Front, in the innocence of his excitement, described how the rig was developed and to be used, she listened with more guilt than gratitude. It was one thing to snooker Sam, but another to take in his boy.

"And here's some fresh ammunition," offered Sam handing her a canister of fresh caught bait hopping and drumming against the lid.

"Well you two don't leave me no excuses," Ojay awkwardly replied. "I'm obliged. Now the rest if up to me."

"Let me know if you do any good." Front was happy to say to her what she had said to him.

"I will," Ojay promised, wishing she didn't have to. What a miserable fix! Between entering the competition and committing this betrayal the entire venture had lost a lot of lustre since the day Mary had pled the justice of her cause. It would be good to get back to the way things were. To how things were supposed to be, where fishing meant no more than catching trout and guile was only used against the fish.

Never one to put off the unpleasant, Ojay locked up behind her visitors and immediately left in search of the Reverend who, it being Friday, was not hard to find and was happy to be interrupted. While he looked forward to the preaching part of his profession, he procrastinated about the preparation, a practice Ojay found hard to understand since he regularly complained about the habit but did nothing to change it.

"Just getting started?" she asked, knowing the answer. She had found him staring out the window of his study, actually the spare bedroom of the small rectory in which he lived.

"You'd think writing a sermon would get easier over the years, but it never seems to," replied the Reverend turning around to greet his accuser.

"No reason why it should. Good things stay hard to do. Like fishing. Like tomorrow. Give a look." And she dropped a couple of Sam's rigs upon the cluttered desk.

The Reverend laid down his pad, grateful for the distraction, and carefully inspected the strange creations.

"Very clever," he pronounced at last. "Part frame, part harness and part noose. Do you notice how he bent the hook? Missed his calling, did Sam. A regular inventor when he puts his mind to it. Have you tried them out?"

"No. But Sam has, and that's good enough for me. Mostly they work, he says. The trick is to keep your line from whipping and the grasshopper from snapping off. You and I, we've got from now 'til dark to rehearse our act one final time and for you to get the feel of casting this contraption. Because come five o'clock tomorrow morning you and MacGregor are due at my place for the real thing. I want us planted in the water below Grisham's Well by six. Then we don't move for half an hour to let the river settle down before we start."

The Reverend signified agreement, taking his marching orders without complaint.

"You get the word to Mac tonight," she continued. "Cut him off at home before he leaves to do his drinking. If he objects, tell him cause Ojay ain't accepting no complaints from the night before as excuses on the morning after. If we fail, it won't be from feeling hung over. Now, let's get some practice while the light still holds."

Obediently the Reverend gathered up his gear and they walked half a mile to the Railroad Shallows, one hundred yards of rippling water glistening in the waning sun, the river's breadth having reduced the depth for easy wading all the way across. Side by side they splashed out to mid stream, Ojay positioning herself by his right side as he stripped the reel and she coiled the line, draping the loops on one hand so she could freely feed the Reverend's cast as he required. Her job was to relieve him of worry about tangles as the line sped out, allowing him to grip the rod with both hands to increase the power of pull and thrust.

They made a good team. The Reverend a man of bachelor regularity to whom habit was order and order peace. Ojay, adaptable to changing circumstance, able to improvise as need arose, gradually secured the Reverend in this new routine by practicing 'til it became familiar.

Adding the third party to their expedition next morning did nothing to improve congeniality on the team since MacGregor bridled under orders not his own and hated being beholden to anyone. Also, his mood was fouled by abstinence the night before. However, since his only chance to beat Sam Henry depended on Ojay and the Reverend, he did his best to keep ill humor under wrap of silence, grunting agreement as she explained their strategy one final time.

"I've done my best by the both of you, but there ain't no middle way. Extremes is what we're stuck with. Reverend, you'll have to throw more line than you can handle. Mac, you'll have to play the fish on much less than you need. Forty feet at most is what you'll have to keep him leashed after the cast is made. And he'll take double that on his first run. Do you have a way to slow him down?"

"I've got three ways," MacGregor grumbled, not about to tip his hand to his confederates, nor did Ojay expect he would.

"You're a secretive man, MacGregor!" the Reverend whispered as they quietly approached the pool. "Do you trust no one? Not even your friends?"

"I trust myself," MacGregor muttered, vexed by the question, irritated he could not give vent to the annoyance he was feeling.

"Not even Mary?" asked Ojay, because it was for Mary she had agreed to do what she was doing now, and she wanted the wife's loyalty reciprocated by the husband, else why was she here?

"Does the left hand trust the right?" exploded MacGregor, stifling the noise, frustrated, not understanding what family had to do with fishing at a time like this. "Now will you leave it alone?"

"Hush!" commanded Ojay. "No more talking!" And she led them into the rapids below Grisham's Well.

Out into the middle of the stream they marched, she stepping aside to let the other two pass by, to her left the Reverend, MacGregor next to him. Once in position, the three shifted their feet until the rocks beneath stopped rolling and each fisherman was firmly anchored in the bottom. Then for the next half hour they stood as still as stumps, the river flowing around them, the mist rising about them, the water chilled by a night of darkness, invigorating their senses with shivers of cold, their eyes straining for visibility in the imperceptibly increasing light.

Dawn at last.

Ojay touched the Reverend on the arm and he began to strip his reel, loop after loop until one hundred and twenty feet of line, the weight of her responsibility hung from her hand. Enough. Now for the bait. Opening the box on his belt the Reverend withdrew the largest of four grasshoppers Ojay had supplied and gently slid the insect into place securing it according to Sam's ingenuity. When the creature successfully flew from his grasp dragging hook and line behind, the Reverend knew he had made the right choice.

Watching the preparation, MacGregor, one hand thrust deep into a trouser pocket, was making a selection of his own.

As they had practiced, so the Reverend and Ojay began. They leaned forward and back in tandem, he with two hands gripping the rod like an athlete, she releasing him line in response to timing he determined as the cast reached further and further upstream, the man now breathing heavy with exertion, but the woman kept relentlessly demanding more. With an exacting eye she measured the closing distance between the insect's forward flight and the destination she required. More casts than he anticipated.

"I can't heave it any further!" the Reverend gasped. "I've never thrown so much line in my life. Not with a fly this heavy!"

"Yes you can!" Ojay encouraged. "Another twenty-five or twenty feet before you shoot the remainder. Come on, keep your line up!"

"I'm trying!" answered the Reverend truthfully, but he was running out of strength to keep so many feet aloft. "I can't increase the line without bringing down the cast." And indeed the cast was barely maintaining, the forward curl lowering, threatening to whip the surface of the water and destroy their plans.

"Come on Reverend!" attacked MacGregor groping for some provocation to inspire extra effort. "Prove your faith. If you can't find strength within yourself then for God's sake, pray for what you need!"

"Pray?" Trading insults was a fair exchange, but this was blasphemy. "MacGregor, you heathen! Prayer's not for worldly wants!" And he thrust his anger into the cast lifting it higher off the water, momentarily relieving MacGregor of anxiety but not frustration. So close and yet so far. He must strike again.

"Father Hypocrite is who you are! Up to your ass in water and acting like you're in the pulpit. Are you too proud to practice what you preach to others?"

Instinctively MacGregor ducked as the cast meant for the fish was nearly meant for him, the grasshopper hissing by, almost nicking his ear, the Reverend changing trajectory intent on drawing blood.

"Pray? The likes of you telling me to pray?" In fury the Reverend began double hauling line up to a greater speed, but not lengthening his cast, preparing his rejoinder.

"Have it your way, MacGregor, and I'll have mine. I make this cast for you today, you be in church for me Sunday next. Agreed?"

"The Hell I will!" MacGregor had not expected to be trapped into a bargain.

"Then the same with your fish!" The Reverend had him caught and both men knew it.

Silence and then submission.

"Agreed! Now get on with it. If you can!"

Ojay got ready. The time for now or never had arrived. MacGregor had accomplished what she could not.

"God help me!" cried out the Reverend in supplication, for the distance was truly beyond him and he knew it. Heaving back, he flung the line behind him then hurled it forward running out another twenty feet, hauling the full length back again and now with one tremendous thrust shot all of that and the remainder straight upstream to reach the spot Ojay selected, slacking the line for just the slightest hesitation, the grasshopper appearing to alight upon the water, the accidental victim of an errant breeze. Even MacGregor had to admit it was a glory of a cast.

"Take it!" The Reverend shoved the rod at MacGregor who took it in his left hand, leaving his right cocked and ready by his side.

The two stepped back to give MacGregor clearance, all three watching as the grasshopper first stretched its wings, crouched down upon the surface then sprang into the air, free at last. Except the water rose up underneath the flying insect in a swell that swallowed the creature down, the sudden surge subsiding in a telltale swirl. The grasshopper was gone.

But it was what came next that most surprised Ojay and the Reverend. Within seconds, the water above where the strike had occurred exploded as though someone was deliberately throwing stones to create disturbance. How MacGregor had learned to drive fish as a boy he had not forgotten as a man, nor had he lost speed of release or accuracy with age.

The trout bolted off at a diagonal from the commotion, more downstream than up, MacGregor recovering precious line needed to remain connected for the fight to follow. Then with giant strides he splashed for shore and charged up the bank, ignoring the underbrush and overgrowth obstructing his path, intent only on keeping his rod clear and cutting down the distance from him that the fish could run. Better to play it from the side of the pool than from the foot. Sapplings gave way before him, branches whipped his face, briars tore his clothes and clawed his skin, but physical discomfort did not seem to matter.

"Don't the man feel damage to his body?" Ojay was appalled by the battering MacGregor was making and taking.

"Not since I've known him," replied the Reverend, "He's never minded pain because his mind won't let him. His body does what he commands it to."

Yet both observers appreciated the point of this abuse, MacGregor had equitized a losing situation.

"At least the fish won't run him out of line," Ojay observed, relieved by how the odds had evened.

"Except he's backed himself into a corner," the Reverend warned. "He can't land the fish from where he is, but he can't retreat without giving up advantage. By outsmarting the fish, he's outsmarted himself. See how he has to reach the rod to keep it from the trees? Lean out any further and he'll be playing the fish from underwater."

It was so. With the trout stubbornly sulking under the opposing bank and no way to lift his rod or move it sideways to encourage the lunker out, MacGregor had become unwilling partner to a standoff. If he didn't extricate himself and provoke the trout to fight, rest would revive what strength the initial run had spent and then no telling what the fish would do.

MacGregor did not underestimate the brown trout's native cunning, crediting its resourcefulness for teaching him much of his own. Over the years competition had created a resemblance, MacGregor learning to use his quarry's tactics against them, himself becoming trout-like in the way he hunted trout. Added to these were principles of his own devising, two of which he called on now: keep the initiative and do the unexpected.

"What in the name of all that's holy!" gasped the Reverend.

"He's run amuck!" echoed Ojay equally astonished.

Neither understood that if MacGregor had gone crazy, it was crazy smart, like a predator certain of his prey.

Leaping off the bank legs pulled up against his chest, MacGregor cannonballed into the river arms raised high, one hand grasping the pole the other gathering in line as he descended through the air. The glass top of the pool was shattered, spray flying up on impact and raining down full thirty feet around as the man plunged in and disappeared, only the tip of the rod periscoping the surface then miraculously rising as MacGregor furiously tread water with his legs, arms and head and shoulders re-emerging, the rod now bent into the fish, the fish becoming startled where it lay.

Puffing like an engine of supreme exertion, chest heaving in and out as legs pumped up and down, the man chugged resolutely through the water toward the trout which, never having been pursued like this before, gave up its sanctuary diving for another, underneath a sunken stump. But the pursuit continued no matter where it fled, driving it from one hiding place into another until it turned to panic and confusion for escape, as MacGregor knew eventually it would. Erratically it started darting in one direction then another only to have MacGregor turn and follow its retreat toward every point upon the compass, but there was no freedom to be found. So it swam the compass round again which was a fatal mistake because now the fish was unwittingly circling the man, and now the man knew he had won. Tightening the circle was only a matter of time. As the trout tired it would draw closer to the center, which it gradually did, losing strength to each wind on the reel, wearily submitting to its master.

Now MacGregor, sure of his catch, lay back in the water and relaxed his kick into a lazy flutter, riding slowly down the current buoyant as a barge, towing the beaten trout behind him, savoring the victory he had earned and the title that would once again be his. Gazing skyward, he rehearsed in his mind how he would break and boast the news to Sam Henry.

By the time he ran aground at the foot of the pool the trout was beyond the point of all resistance and slipped obediently into the net Ojay held waiting. Hefting the prize aloft for all three to admire she announced her verdict.

"You've beat Sam's fish by half a pound or better!"

"Congratulations, Mac!" The Reverend clapped him on the shoulder. "You've saved the title for the town. I guess we all have."

"Even Sam," Ojay added. "Designed his own defeat."

"Naw!" objected MacGregor. "He rigged the bait, that's all. The three of us, we caught the trout."

"You caught the trout, you mean," the Reverend corrected. "Chased it and caught it. I'll say this for you, Mac. You're not a man who heeds the orthodoxies when it comes to fishing."

"I do whatever it takes," MacGregor admitted. "You don't break records by obeying rules."

"Still," argued the Reverend, "Ojay's right. Sam had a hand in your success. You've got to give him credit."

MacGregor smiled.

"I mean to thank him proper when we meet. And enjoy the look upon his face."

"Yes," said the Reverend. "No doubt he'll take it hard. But I'll go you one better, Mac. Seeing your face in church next Sunday."

"What? So you'd hold me to that, would you?"

"I would and I do," replied the Reverend sternly, not about to let a big one get away. "Before witnesses you gave your word. Or is your word only a matter of convenience?"

Ojay shook her head. They were back at it again.

"My word?" huffed MacGregor. "At least I don't use words to preach at others! I suppose you'll write a sermon just for me?"

"I suppose I will."

"No doubt the subject's one you have in mind?" scoffed MacGregor, bitter at the thought.

"No doubt," the Reverend now as sure of his catch as MacGregor had been of his. "I thought I'd start at the beginning just for you. In Genesis. Do you know the story of Noah, Mac?"

"What difference?" growled MacGregor. "I guess I'll know it well enough before you're through."

"I'll do my best," the Reverend promised.

"Your worst, you mean!"

"Come on the two of you," Ojay interrupted, weary of their bickering. If this was friendship between men, she was glad she was a woman. "The longer you stand and quarrel, your fish out of water, the lighter it will weigh on Wally's scale."

Warning enough for MacGregor. Let the Reverend do his damnedest next Sunday. Today was for the Trout King. And for celebration.

CHAPTER TEN

BETRAYAL AND DISCOVERY

As luck would have it, and luck always did, Sam and Front were checking out their weekend groceries when the three fishermen paraded into Detmer's, MacGregor in the lead followed by a crowd of locals eager for a second look.

"Well, Sam!" declaimed MacGregor raising his voice above the row. "To think I should have you to thank!"

At first, Sam only saw the sudden throng.

"Whatever for?" he asked, innocent of the commotion.

"For this!" MacGregor lifted high the trout to the accompaniment of cheers.

Sam's face darkened in disappointment, then lit up in admiration.

"Congratulations, Mac! I thought I'd caught the biggest fish in the river, but you found one bigger."

"Ojay, you mean." corrected MacGregor. "She found it in Grisham's Well. Thrown for another fifty feet and you might have caught it yourself!"

"What?" asked Sam amazed. "In Grisham's Well? Two that size in the same pool? So long a cast? I didn't think you had the distance in you Mac."

"I didn't," confessed MacGregor, pleased to reveal the full extent of the conspiracy. "The Reverend here made the cast of his everlasting life."

"It's true, Sam," the Reverend replied. "It took all three of us. Even then MacGregor had to jump into the drink to play the lunker out."

Now Sam noticed how MacGregor was soaking wet. He grinned.

"Well, Mac, that would have been a baptism worth witnessing. I wish I'd been there."

"You were there, Sam. You were. In a manner of speaking. We couldn't have done it without you," laughed MacGregor in huge enjoyment of his joke.

Sam looked confused which pleased MacGregor even more. Now for the stunner.

"It was your lure we caught this beauty on!"

Front, whose attention had been fixed on the trout heavily hanging from MacGregor's upraised hand, jerked around to face his father who was facing Ojay.

"So our rig did work?" asked Sam, wanting the answer to come from her.

"To perfection," responded Ojay in praise sincerely meant. Then in apology, "I did it for the town, Sam. I hope you won't take it personal."

Quick to forgive and so avoid resentment, Sam immediately looked on the bright side, as he always did. First addressing Ojay.

"None taken. At least you proved our idea out." Then speaking to his son, "Well Front, they may have got mine beat, but it took the two of us to help them do it."

But Front was in no mood for forgiveness. Why was he feeling angry and his father not? He glared at Ojay.

"So you did good?" The boy's question was intended as an accusation.

Ojay accepted her guilt in his eyes and in her own, telling him what truth she could.

"Sometimes good is bad and bad is good. This here is one of those."

No consolation to Front.

"My mother was right! She said we shouldn't trust you!" This charge as much against his father as Ojay. "It isn't fair!"

"Fair?" scoffed MacGregor. "Then let this be a lesson to you. All's fair in love and war and fishing. Beat is beat no matter how it's done!" He didn't like the boy taking center stage. "Wally! Weigh me in and give Mr. Henry back his little trout to carry home."

"It's not a little trout!" The insult had ignited Front's temper. "And yours is not the biggest in the river. Not for sure."

"And I suppose you'll catch one bigger?" mocked MacGregor.

"If only I could," vowed Front, "I'd give up fishing for the rest of my life!"

"Don't swear what you don't mean," taunted MacGregor, a demonic gleam in his eye.

"Enough of this, Mac!" warned Sam, seeing his son about to make a Devil's Bargain.

Too late. Front had succumbed to the temptation.

"I swear it! I'd give up fishing forever to catch a bigger fish than yours!"

Now Sam stepped in between his son and MacGregor to place the rivalry back where it belonged.

"Leave Front out of the competition between us, Mac. Not just for his sake. For your own. He's more of a fisherman than you suppose."

"A boy! Since when has a boy been competition to a man?" derided MacGregor at the absurdity of such a thought.

"Since David slew Goliath," interjected the Reverend trying to bring the swell of victory down.

To no avail.

"You can bible me a week from Sunday, Reverend. Not before!"

But by now Sam provoked beyond endurance, dashed MacGregor's exultation with a sobering possibility.

"Without this boy's idea your grasshopper would have been dead in the water, your chance for this fish no better. Front had the power to help you today, Mac. Maybe he'll have the power to beat you tomorrow. Or he and I together. Yours is not the only team in town. Either way, the game is over. You want a real run for the title? Well now you've got it!"

Feeling attacked in his moment of triumph by friend and foe alike, MacGregor realized he had overstepped his bounds and worse, by doing so, had created in the son a rival as dedicated as the father. Inwardly, MacGregor cursed the human nature that betrayed him, once again emotion impelling him to act heedless of consequence. He had been led by impulse all his life and it had served him well and badly. Well, when it emboldened him to dare what calm consideration would forbid. Badly, when he had not foreseen the error of a reckless deed or hot blooded words. Mary, she forgave. Sam, easy going was easily mended. But this boy, still glaring, was unforgiving and implacable.

Now trying to conciliate the son through the father, MacGregor retracted criticism he had given.

"No discredit to your catch Sam. Any other year you would have won with a trout this size."

"You're talking like the contest's over, Mac," replied Sam meaning every word. "But it's not. We have over a month to go. The most productive month if August rains come early. Why who knows what kind of luck a summer flood can bring?"

"That's right," Front stoutly agreed, grateful his father showed no sign of giving up.

Now MacGregor repented of his boast. He had meant to discourage further competition, not encourage more. His face soured in disgust.

Wally to the rescue. On whispered orders from Cora, who feared a loss of business from further argument, Wally presented Sam his frozen trout with one hand and, as though chaining partners in a country dance, led MacGregor away with the other to the scales at the back of the store.

"Whoever guesses the closest weight gets a free soda!" challenged Cora, exciting the crowd into following along, voices shouting out their wagers.

Alone by the entrance, each with a bag of groceries cradled in his arms, remained Sam and Front. Alone, but not unnoticed.

Loyal to her post, Mrs. Detmer had closely observed the proceedings from behind the cash register and disapproved the outcome left standing before her --two unhappy customers who might become reluctant to return. Wally's contest was clearly getting out of hand. Meant to be good for business it was turning bad. And Sam a loyal customer. She must remedy the situation if she could.

"What would the Bishop make of all this foofarraw, do you suppose?" she asked, invoking that old topic of speculation between them, hoping in response Sam could ease whatever hurt he and the boy received.

"Too worldly for his tastes, I suspect," Sam replied. "Not for ours though. Not for Front's and mine. No, Mrs. D, MacGregor had his way with us today, but turnabout is fair play. We gave him the lure. Now he's given us incentive. Right Front?"

Mrs. Detmer saw the boy's face brighten with fresh determination and felt relieved of worry while her husband, holding open the door, only felt more foreboding when a roar of voices broke like thunder behind father and son as Mr. Detmer showed them out. Voices acclaiming the official weight of MacGregor's fish and him the winner. Storm warning of trouble ahead.

"Mr. Henry," the older man touched the younger on the arm. "I hope you won't hold what was said inside against the town."

Sam stopped to answer Mr. Detmer's concern.

"Not against the town, Mr. D. Nor against Ojay, the Reverend and MacGregor for throwing in to beat me. As for MacGregor crowing victory, why if it was me, I'd be crowing over him. But for what he said to Front? I've got a score to settle with him there. And if I can strip him of the title to do it, I will."

Mr. Detmer made one final effort at persuasion.

"Settling one grudge by creating another, Mr. Henry. Where will it end?"

"With a winner and a loser, Mr. D. With one man lording it over the other. Or maybe a boy over a man." Then turning to his son, "Come on Front. We've got work to do."

Lowering himself down into his chair, Mr. Detmer slowly rocked back and forth solemnly watching Sam and Front drive away driven closer together by the common sense of purpose they now shared.

Inside the car the two were already making plans.

"Dark places, deep holes and dense cover, Front. That's where to look. Where our eyes can't reach or we see but don't suspect."

"Do you think there is such a fish?" asked Front. "Really? Maybe Mr. MacGregor's was the biggest trout Ojay could find. The biggest there is."

"Maybe so," agreed Sam. "It sure is a walloper. But being experts doesn't mean she and MacGregor know it all. Remember, they may have knowledge of the river on their side, but we've got the advantage of ignorance on ours."

"Not much of an advantage," replied Front glumly.

"More than you suppose. Knowing so little you and I will be looking everywhere, while knowing so much they'll just search the spots they think worthwhile. That's our edge, in trying places they ignore. We may discover what they overlook."

Front was unpersuaded, but willing. He didn't share his father's chronic optimism. However, he was not about to take defeat without a fight.

When they got home Estelle acted unsurprised by the news of MacGregor's winning catch. Although she didn't say 'I told you so,' father and son both felt the silent sting of her reproof. All the encouragement each needed to gather up their gear and head off for different stretches of the river, leaving Estelle feeling hurt for her son and angry at her husband.

Never had Front approached fishing with such deliberation. Never had he waded more carefully, scanned the surface more closely, searched beneath it more intently. And in doing so he recognized the river for what it was, an adversary as wiley as the trout that hid in its clear waters. Transparency was not to be trusted because light was naturally deceptive, creating illusions that continually tricked his eyes. Sunlit shallows turned deeper than he had initially supposed, while shadow implied depth which upon closer inspection proved not deep at all.

Appearance was rarely what it seemed, only an elaborate pretense that favored fish over fisherman. There were so many subtle places for a trout to find concealment, but where was a fisherman to hide? Particularly on an afternoon so bright that even the nylon leader cast a shadow as it floated over the river bottom below.

Front was getting tired. It was hard work. One small trout for all his efforts, yet some surprising finds he would remember. Holes had been discovered he had not known about before, so time was not entirely wasted. Time for a rest was how he felt. Up ahead, aglare in the sunlight, was the bend of the river.

Since the spot was forever unyielding of fish, in the past few years he had begun to put it to another use – as a swimming pool to escape the summer heat. This he had done on a number of occasions, slipping into the headwaters, the rapids sweeping him along the rock face until at last he ran aground where the river shallowed out, the ride cooling his body and exciting his spirit of adventure. Challenging himself he would swim up against the current and then surface dive straight down holding his breath to bursting in hopes of touching bottom, but he never did. The pool was deep beyond his knowing, while the further he descended the dimmer light became, shadows of branches and other sunken shapes frightening his imagination as he fled for daylight and for air, exhilarated by the sense of danger, doing it again.

He had told his father about the wreckage of trees and of hollows worn into the rock, dark recesses into which he could not see. He had described the excitement of his fear, could feel the same excitement building now as he approached the pool, a wonderfully scary place of his own making.

Perhaps emboldened by commitment to the contest or by his brazen vow to Mr. MacGregor, Front felt an urge to enhance his risk by daring something new. His eyes naturally climbed up the steep rock to the top where a few stubby fir trees managed to root a living out of cracks in the age old stone. Suppose, instead of easing into the headwaters, he jumped down from the rock. Would the fall take him deeper than his usual dive? But he couldn't scale the granite face. He would have to circle around and find a way up from behind. Then the jump. No more than fifteen feet. No less. He began to feel the thrill of apprehension. Challenge accepted.

So, forsaking his usual approach, he left the river below the pool. Laying his creel and rod between the roots of a large tree, he stripped off his shirt and removed his shoes, and picked his way through the tangle of growth to the backside of what was one enormous boulder, refuse by some bygone glacier from some prehistoric time.

Scrambling up and over the hard surface, finding purchase with his fingers and his toes, Front soon reached the summit, out of breath from the swift climb, heart pounding even faster when, looking down, he realized how much higher he felt than he had calculated from below. Leaping off now required further thought and the gathering of courage, so he sat down to reconsider and recover his wind.

Looking to his left and then to his right he could see both up and down the river. Leaning forward, the smooth current lay glistening between his feet. For a while he stared absently at the running water, letting his eyes become fascinated by the shifting curls of current, then by something beneath the surface waving out from an indentation in the rock. A branch with large leaves. Then it disappeared. That's funny. There it was again. Now he focused his eyes more clearly. Not a branch. Those weren't leaves. It almost looked like the tail fin of some enormous fish. He smiled and looked away. The contest must be getting to him. Wishful thinking on a grand scale. Then he looked back. There it was again. What was it?

Something started crawling up his leg. It was a large black beetle apparently blind to the difference between a boy and a rock. Front picked it off and without thinking flicked it over the edge landing it about ten feet from where he had been gazing.

Then unreality appeared.

Front could not believe his eyes. Out from the hollow in the rock materialized a fish by breadth and length beyond the boy's wildest imaginings. A giant trout it was. A brown trout it must be since no other kind, according to his father, grow so large. Only for a moment did the great gray shape hang beneath the stranded insect when, perhaps sensing its jeopardy, the beetle burst into a flurry of activity vanishing the fish before Front could see it leave.

What had happened unhappened so swiftly Front found himself staring at vacant water, the beetle swept downstream, the fish, if indeed a fish there was, erased from view. The boy shook his head to clear his head and let reality back in when evidence of unreality appeared again – the huge tail waving in the current just clear of the rock. Evidence too telling to deny. Seeing became believing. Staring became a way to affirm his improbable conviction.

How long Front sat there, he could not say. It was a long time, however, because when he recovered his attention sufficiently to raise his eyes, shadows had already begun to fall about him.

What was he going to do? What in the world was he going to do? A hundred flies he'd floated by this rock at every time of day and the fish had never given one of them a turn. At most it may have looked them over like it did the beetle. But the fish didn't take the beetle. Why? Surely a tiny insect couldn't scare such an enormous trout by simply stirring up the water. Or was the trout grown so suspicious it would take nothing unless absolutely sure?

Maybe if he dropped a fly down from above. At least he could try. But how could he land the fish from so high? Couldn't haul it up without breaking it off. Couldn't climb down without breaking himself. Even if he could, his line was not strong enough to stop a run into that deep tangle of underwater branches and escape. Front's mind became an intense debate of opposing ideas. What he suggested on the one hand he would dismiss on the other, confirming again and again the impossibility of hooking and landing such a great fish in such hazardous surroundings.

Out of curiosity he searched for another bug, finding underneath a loosened flap of moss a worm like insect with many legs that he tossed into the river where he had accidentally thrown the beetle before. This time he only succeeded in scaring the trout off entirely. The great tail did not reappear.

Got to go home, he sighed, standing up, stretching his cramped muscles. His body thirsted for a swim more than ever. Hot and stiff from the afternoon's excitement, he longed to jump into the water but he resisted the cool temptation. This pool was not for swimming anymore. It was for fishing only. For only one special fish.

Clambering back down the boulder proved more difficult than climbing up. His legs were unsteady and he felt light-headed. Then he remembered he had not eaten much since breakfast. Anger, excitement, and hunger had depleted his energy over the course of the long day. Stooping to retrieve his fishing rod, stuffing his shirt and shoes into his creel, he took a parting glance at the pool. Such a perfect spot! He and his father had often discussed the frustration of it. The man's verdict: "A real heartbreaker. Idyllic looking and absolutely unproductive. Just leaves you crying at the alter."

What would his father say now? How would he tell his father? How could words convince? They couldn't.

Inside the creel hugging against his hip he felt the slight bulge of the single trout – barely a keeper – he had caught earlier. What had pleased him at the time now caused him to feel foolish. Even ashamed for taking pride in a fish so small compared to the prize he had discovered. The scale of his expectations had irrevocably changed. Sight of the great trout had given him a great challenge and caused a significant loss as well. Nothing less would ever satisfy again. He trudged on home.

"Do any good?" asked his father as the boy walked in.

"No. Yeah. I got one." Front slid the trout into the sink and began cleaning it, slitting open the belly, pulling out the entrails, rinsing the empty cavity with water.

"Well you did better than me. I got skunked." Confessed Sam noticing the subdued nature of his son's response. "You okay?"

"Yes. Except something happened today I need to tell you about."

"I'm listening."

"No." Front changed his mind. "I can't tell you about it. I need to show you. Will you come with me tomorrow morning?"

"Sure. You all right? You get into some kind of trouble? MacGregor again? His sons?"

"No. Not them." Front didn't want his father to get the wrong idea. "I did get into something. Not trouble. At least I don't think it is. More like a problem."

"Sounds like a mystery."

"In a way," replied Front seriously. "Maybe you can solve it."

Sam would have liked more information but understood from his son's reticence none would be forthcoming.

At supper they talked about extraneous things, Estelle avoiding the sore point of MacGregor's fish, the two men glad not to bring it up. Both Sam and Estelle wished she had not been right. But by the topic's noticeable absence, it was clear all three were thinking of little else. The meal over, they felt relieved from the strain of acting awkward with each other, awkwardness between the parents that beset the son when routine forced them to be family together.

Front wished this were not so. He wished his parents had some way to bridge the differences between them, some way to share with each other what each shared with him – Sam, his love of fishing, taking expeditions on the river; Estelle, her love of books, reading aloud to Front in bed at night. But his parents were no longer interested in each other.

Sometimes, increasingly in recent times, Front felt he was the only link between his parents. Without him they would pull apart. A scary thought and a heavy responsibility. His job was keeping them connected when it was easier to be separately with each. Easier for his parents, if they had to be together, to have him present, their son the one commonality no amount of intimate estrangement could deny.

It was early to bed for everyone. All were too tired to relax with their usual pursuits. Next morning, Front and his father were up early, setting off right after breakfast.

"Where are we going?" asked Sam. "Or can't you tell me that either?"

"To the pool at the bend of the river," answered Front.

"You been doing some more underwater exploring?" His son's confidence in water always impressed Sam since it far exceeded his own.

"Not exactly. We'll need to go a different way before we get there."

Obediently the man followed the boy's lead.

"Now this is where we leave the river," announced Front. "Through this brush then up that rock. Look around for a beetle as we walk. We'll need one."

"A beetle." Repeated Sam flatly, knowing he was supposed to act unsurprised. Then unable to resist pricking his son's seriousness, he asked equally seriously "male or female?"

"It doesn't matter." Front missed the point. "Never mind, I've found one." He stuffed something in his pocket.

"Good. We need anything else you be sure to let me know."

Again ignoring his father's attempt at humor, Front gave final instructions.

"When we get to the top of the rock be very quiet and don't knock anything into the water."

"Okay. I know you wouldn't ask me to risk life and limb climbing up here without a good reason. Is there a good reason?"

But Front was already scrambling up ahead so Sam, taking what precautions he could, stopped talking and concentrated on finding the best hand and foot holds he could. Reaching the top at last, he sat down to catch his breath, perspiration on his face evaporating in the breeze.

"You win," conceded Sam. "Not only do you enjoy diving deeper than me, you also like climbing higher. Never would have thought to come this way myself. The view, is that what you wanted to show me?"

Front had been peering over the edge.

"Down there. Be very quiet and look down there. See anything?"

Sam looked.

"The water."

"In the water," urged Front.

Sam stared hard trying to see anything out of the ordinary.

"Nothing particular except a branch waving back and forth. Looks like a big fish tail."

"Yes, that."

"What about it?" asked Sam.

"Suppose it really was a fish tail?"

"Well," laughed Sam, "meaning no disrespect, if this rock were solid gold we'd be rich men. But it's not. Anymore than whatever that is belongs to a fish. If it did, you would have found the grand daddy of all trout."

"Watch this," announced Front. Rummaging into his pocket and retrieving the beetle, the boy tossed it down into the water.

Feeling witness to some experiment he did not understand Sam now gave the falling insect his full attention. He did not know what he was expected to observe, but clearly he was supposed to watch closely.

It landed upright, barely penetrating the placid surface, held still, and nothing happened. Sam was about to look away when to his wondering eyes out from beneath them, out from the hollow in the rock, loomed the great trout, hung there for a long moment, then was gone.

"What, what in the name of God was that?" Sam gave vent to the shock he was feeling. "Can't be a fish. Can't be! Did you see the girth on that animal? As big around as a tree! What's it doing here anyway? Fish that size belong in the ocean, not in some little land locked stream." He was shaking all over with excitement. "Not another pool in the whole river deep enough to hold it." Turning to Front, "Do you know what you've found here? The One, that's what. The One and Only. The First and the Last. Right here in our own back yard! Looks big enough to swallow a small dog. Maybe that's what we should have been fishing with all these years – Scotties and Cocker Spaniels." For once Sam's capacity for expression was insufficient to describe his feelings. He fell silent, truly at a loss for words.

"How would you try to catch it?" asked Front.

"I don't know," considered Sam, baffled by the question. "Something so enormous in a fortress like this pool. With all these protections around him? I don't know. To be honest, I'm not sure this trout is catchable. At least not on the terms you and I ordinarily fish. What comes immediately to mind is poison or explosives, not exactly congenial approaches for us. And no guarantee even those would work on a behemoth like this. Now MacGregor, he'd find a way. MacGregor! Front, if he knew, he'd kill to get a fish like this. Or at least kill to keep someone else from catching it. Trout King? Whoever lands this monster can retire the title!"

"You're not going to tell him?" asked Front anxiously.

"Heck no! He's got his secrets, now we've got ours."

"So how do we catch it?" Front repeated his question, determined to get his father's collaboration.

Sam bit his thumb in thought.

"Even assuming we could get him to take some manner of fly, I don't know how we'd hold him. Besides, just thinking about hooking him gives me Buck Fever."

"What's that?" Front had never heard the term before.

"Buck Fever? It's kind of disabling excitement hunters occasionally get when they finally have a trophy deer right in their gun sights. Suddenly their entire body freezes up. They can't move muscle enough to squeeze the trigger. Not 'til after the prize has walked away. The frustration of it is enough to make a grown man cry. It happens to fishermen too. I know, cause it happened once to me. A long time ago I was plugging for northern pike up in one of those still Canadian lakes, casting a spoon from a canoe into reed beds that lined the shore."

"How come you never told me?"

"Wasn't hiding it. It just never came to mind. 'Til now. Remember it like yesterday. Water so clear I could see the lure coming toward me as soon as I began retrieving it. Then from out of no where charges this pike that looks like a cross between a large torpedo and a small submarine. Cruising right after my red and white spoon. All I had to do was keep reeling in to get a solid strike. That's when it hit."

"The pike?"

"Buck fever." Sam's voice dropped. "Soon as I realized that what I wanted more than anything was within reach, my body stiffened up. I couldn't move my hand. Couldn't even lift a finger. Darnedest act of self-sabotage you ever saw. All I could do was watch my spoon stop dead and flutter to the bottom. The pike stopped too. We both just watched that misguided piece of metal go down. Then the fish swam off and I felt sick to my stomach. Trembling and faint. Of course command of my body came right back, but by then it was too late. Buck Fever. Catch it once and you remember it for the rest of your life." Sam shuddered to shake off the memory.

One more time Front brought the conversation round to the problem at hand.

"How would you catch this fish?"

Sam smiled at his son's persistence.

"Well, first off, I wouldn't. This is your fish, not mine. It was given to you to find, so if an attempt on its life is going to be made, you need to be the one to make it. However, if you want a partner in crime, count me in."

"So you have some ideas?"

"No. Not yet. Not offhand. But just because I'm fresh out at the moment doesn't mean I won't have one in stock tomorrow. You and I, we've got some deep thinking to do. Just remember, no idea is too far fetched to fool a fish like this into taking a fly, much less fighting him to shore. We'll figure something!" And Sam clapped his son on the back, one team mate to another. "We have to. Because if the devious minds of two experienced fishermen aren't a match for the greatest trout of all time, then you and I better put away our fishing poles and take up some less demanding form of recreation."

"And MacGregor? Suppose he finds this fish?"

"He won't. If he hasn't yet, he won't. Mac's too fixed in his beliefs to change his mind. Too full of his own prowess to imagine himself wrong for writing off this spot. No, the one I worry about is Wally."

"Why?" Front did not understand.

"Because," laughed Sam, "he's going to have to invest in a bigger scale to weigh this fish. And knowing Cora, she won't be happy approving the expense."

CHAPTER ELEVEN

THE CELEBRATION'S REVENGE

After Sam and Front had departed Detmer's, hurrahs from MacGregor's victory resounding through the open door behind them, the victor himself, full of himself and thirsty for more, led his most ardent admirers down the street to the Tavern where they could celebrate with something more suitable than soda.

There, leaning back against the bar, regaling an audience of well-wishers, MacGregor kept embellishing the story of his winning, improving the tale with each retelling, as his best friends of the moment competed with each other to buy him drinks because in doing so they bought themselves some small share in his glory. MacGregor had won, the town had won, and they had won, each and everyone, so all deserved congratulations. It was a riotous good time, good feelings enhanced with a good drink, the call of the family at last diminishing the crowd as the afternoon wore on and dinner time drew nigh.

Last to go, MacGregor did not like to celebrate alone, but neither would he quit before pledging his fill. And he wanted more. So, driving erratically for home, he idealized the reception that awaited. He would be treated as a conquering hero bringing honor to his family. But things went wrong.

Braking sharply to avoid hitting a broken generator left disassembled at the end of the rutted drive, he was thrown across the wheel banging his head against the windshield, abruptly turning angry, cursing whoever had strewn the wreckage there, forgetting it was himself. What welcome was this?

It was the sound of a car too fast approaching that first caught Mary's attention, then peering through the kitchen window the sight of MacGregor reeling and squealing his battered vehicle to a brutal stop, whipping the man forward and back hard enough to cause him hurt, hurt enough to make a hard homecoming. She knew the signs, and this was worse than usual. A good thing women did not give in to drinking like men, although at times like this even she felt tempted.

Knowing what to do, she did what she had done so many times before, and ordered the boys to stay out back 'til she had calmed their father. Then she would call them in for supper. By now they understood.

She waited at the window watching for MacGregor to come in, growing more uneasy when he did not. While MacGregor waited for Mary to come out, growing more angry when she did not. Damn the woman! Was his well-being of no concern? But Mary learned long ago not to insult his pride by tending to his injuries, having been cursed for caring when she had tried before.

At last, fed up with her neglect and impatient to share his news, MacGregor kicked open the door, tumbled out, tripped over his feet, and pitched up against the porch, grabbing the rail to keep from falling down, squeezing tight to clear his head and restore his balance.

Mary stepped out.

"Do you want supper?" she asked, apparently oblivious to his condition.

"Supper!" he bellowed. "I want a feast! But first I want my sons!"

Free standing up now, he stood steady on his legs, the ground no longer heaving underfoot.

"Bring me my sons!" MacGregor ordered. "I have something to say. To all of you!"

Mary did not protest. When he was argumentative she knew better than to argue back.

"Wait here," she evenly replied and retreated into the house to fetch the boys, instructing them not to talk back lest they inflame their father's temper. They obeyed.

MacGregor watched with eager anticipation as his wife and sons filed out onto the porch. This was more like what he wanted, an audience of family to applaud his triumph. Telling was too easy. First. he would make them wonder, then make them guess.

"Well Gordie, Goeff! Well, Mary! And who's the talk of the town today? And why do you suppose?" MacGregor sought to wet their appetite with curiosity for what he had to share.

None of the three dared say, each imagining some new embarrassment publicly being told against the family on his behalf. The thought that something good occurred never entered their minds and so, finding nothing affirmative to offer, they were silent, the last response MacGregor wanted to receive.

"Well don't be shy," urged MacGregor impatiently. "Speak up! You, Goeff, why do you suppose the town's astir about your father, eh?"

As was his habit when interrogated thus, Goeff looked to his brother to reply. But MacGregor, in no mood for evasion, held fast to what he wanted.

"It's you I'm asking, Goeff. Gordie, be still!"

"MacGregor," interrupted Mary, "say your piece, then we can eat."

"You too Mary!" warned MacGregor. He was not to be denied. This was his occasion and he would have it his way. First they would guess wrong. Then he would set them right. Then they would lavish him with praise.

"Well, boy?" and MacGregor lurched up the stairs arms reaching out to grab from Goeff what was not given, to shake loose the words withheld, when Gordie planted himself in between, two steps above his father, on eye level with the man.

"Leave him be, Da," objected Gordie. "He doesn't know what you want. No more do I."

MacGregor stopped his climb, one train of thought now broken by another, what he wanted instantly supplanted by what he must assert.

"Are you challenging your father again, Gordie?" and MacGregor's eyes grew bright with pleasure and hard with resolve. "Is it Man of the House you want to play?"

"Stop it!" pleaded Mary who saw what was coming and hated what she saw. The game of father against son learned from his father that MacGregor dutifully had taught the boys. Except only one was willing. Gordie goes up against his father to be like his father. Goeff refused what resemblance he could by acting opposite in every way.

"Who's Man of the House?" demanded MacGregor, backing up his invitation by backing down the steps making room for his son to follow, which Gordie did, the two now facing off across the circle of hard ground that spread before the porch.

Normally Gordie loved doing battle with his father because he loved his father and the man would regulate his roughness in proportion to the resistance given by the son. So although occasionally bruised, Gordie felt in control of the fight if not the outcome that was assured, since the man was bound to win. But this time the game was played with a difference. Gordie had deliberately opposed his father's rule, while his father instead of fighting sober was fighting drunk.

This difference was not lost upon Mary, nor how the game had changed over the years. At first it had been father and child wrestling for a pin, then Gordie growing into boyhood standing toe to toe, who could push the hardest, who could keep his feet. Until last year when, showing signs of early manhood on his body, Gordie would not be shoved off balance so blows were exchanged, punches pulled but punches also taken to prove who could knock down whom. Who was dominant. MacGregor every time.

Now the two began weaving toward each other, Gordie adopting the crouch learned from his father. MacGregor eyeing his adversary with angry approval, determined to teach his older son a lesson and to teach him well.

Looking on, Goeff was filled with fear and admiration for his brother who had taught him how to fight by beating him if he did not fight back. At times an older brother felt like a second father, harsher in some ways than the first but also more protective. Paying the price for protecting him now.

It was MacGregor made the first feint that Gordie reached to parry leaving himself wide open for his father's other fist delivering a hammer blow against his chest, staggering the boy back several steps to keep from falling over, the pain convincing him this was no ordinary play. Having disobeyed his mother's instruction and his father's command, he must bear the consequence without backing down.

"It's like a shell game, Boy," MacGregor taunted as he taught. "Which fist has the punch? Pick the wrong one and you'll get the other."

Enter Mary. She had witnessed enough. This was no game that she could see or stand to see. This was a mismatch meant for doing harm. Unless Gordie lay down, which she knew he would not. Like his father, he'd be killed before he'd quit. So she must call it quits for them by giving pride an out.

"Enough MacGregor. I can't take any more!" Mary blamed herself for cowardice in hopes they'd stop the fight for her if not themselves.

But MacGregor was not to be dissuaded.

"Then look away, woman. I'm only teaching the boy how to take up for himself."

Now Mary grabbed MacGregor from behind.

"Stop it, I say! Let Gordie be! I won't have him hurt!"

Just as MacGregor reached around to pry Mary off his back, Gordie landed his one and only blow deep into his father's stomach, winding the man, causing him to gasp and grasp the nature of what just occurred.

"So that's the game, is it?" MacGregor charged, outraged by the fearful answer threatening his mind. "Two against one. Taking sides. Choosing your son over your husband!" The old blood jealousy affirmed. "Get thee away!" and with a sweep of his arm he flung her back against the porch and turned to finish the fight that having sons had started.

"Now Boy, I guess we're evened up," conceded MacGregor shuffling to his right causing Gordie to pivot left to face his father, the boy thrown slightly off balance by this maneuver. MacGregor's intent.

"You want to fight to keep the other at a disadvantage," the man instructed, "to keep the openings in your favor. Do you understand?"

Gordie nodded. Listening had distracted him from looking. The opening MacGregor wanted. Too late the boy saw his mistake. The first blow knocked him off his feet, the second hastened his fall, and the third, not from his father but hardest of all, was delivered by the packed ground crashing against his head. Stunned by the impact Gordie lay still until his vision cleared enough to recognize his father's hand extended to help him up. Dumbly he accepted his assistance, was pulled to standing, then struck down before he could defend himself.

"That will teach you to trust help from an opponent," scorned MacGregor for whom stupidity in combat was a cardinal sin. "Now have you learned enough?"

On all fours not yet able to arise, still groggy, Gordie shook his head, willingness to fight his father back not yet subdued.

"What?" asked MacGregor. "I didn't hear!"

His mouth too liquid filled and swollen to speak clearly, Gordie mumbled a response his father could not understand.

"Give up, speak up, or stand up!" commanded MacGregor. "Now once and for all, who's the Man of the House?"

But Gordie was not about to pay attention to his father's words. They had betrayed him once. He did not trust them anymore. Besides, he had an enemy far worse to fight: himself. He hurt so bad the hurt was everywhere. He felt so weak he lacked the strength to move. His beaten body craved surrender. But his mind refused. Will opposed won't and won, the agonizing victory apparent to MacGregor who watched in wonder as rung by painful rung Gordie slowly pulled himself upright.

It showed more courage than MacGregor could withstand. Anger gave way to admiration. Admiration to pride. What a son! To have fathered such a son!

"Give it up Boy," urged MacGregor gently, lowering his arms. "You've done yourself proud. And me. Be done."

Not possible. Gordie had pushed himself too far to turn back now. Arms half limp and half lifted, he stared at the place his father stood. No telling who or what he saw. Perhaps the image of his father as himself.

While Mary, from where she had been thrust aside, beheld continuation of what must be stopped, dumb courage confronting sure defeat to dreadful consequence. Acting to save her son, she nearly got him killed.

"MacGregor!" she screamed. "Harm Gordie further and you'll never touch me again!" The worst threat she could think of. Worse than she knew.

Appreciation of his son's heroics gave way to maddening fear. The woman was prepared to deny her husband to defend her son. Mary's warning had broken admiration's spell. Instantly Gordie was changed from worthy adversary into dreaded foe and MacGregor, protecting what was his right of marriage, smote his rival down, beating his son into submission. Worse, into submissiveness.

Consciousness was lost. And memory for the moment of what occurred. Time was interrupted. Silence filled the void. Then a siren shriek of alarm brought MacGregor to his senses. Something must have happened. What? What happened? He looked curiously around, at first saw nothing. Then noticed Gordie splayed across the ground, his head at an odd angle. Concerned the man bent down to see what ailed his son.

"Don't touch him!" Dimly MacGregor barely heard the noise of Mary shrieking in his face. Straightening up he faintly felt her fists pummeling his chest, pushing him away. She was upset.

"It's all right Mary," murmured MacGregor. "Gordie will be all right," he reassured, allowing her to shove him back.

"Goeff, grab his feet," ordered Mary in distraught command. "We'll carry him inside."

Between the two, mother and son, they hoisted the slack body up the steps, lugged it into the house, and gently lowered it to rest on Gordie's bed, Mary arranging her son for comfort, turning his head back how it belonged.

"Gordie!" she crooned, luring him back from far away, from a place where no one could hurt anybody any more. "Gordie speak to your mother," pleading for his return. No answer. She kept calling until something in her voice connected. Gordie slightly responding, opening his eyes, smiling up at his mother, at his brother, then drifting back into what resembled sleep or some such altered state.

"Thank God!" whispered Mary in gratitude and began to pray, driving Goeff from her side because he hated prayer for the suffering that it endured.

Out in the front yard MacGregor, all alone, was trying to reconstruct what had transpired. Puzzled, he remembered the good news he brought home to tell. Why had he not told it? What had gone wrong?

Edging out the screen door, Goeff quietly sidled over to the corner of the porch, warily watching his father.

Goeff! MacGregor saw it all. It was because of Goeff! He was the one! The one who had refused him satisfaction.

"You, Goeff!" MacGregor called down this son. A reckoning was what he wanted. "Not like your brother, are you?" he accused, expecting no reply.

"No, Da," answered Goeff, his speech uninflected and controlled.

MacGregor was surprised.

"So," he gibed, eager to provoke his son, but only provoking his own anger, "you've lost your brother's voice and found your own, is that it?"

"Yes," came the minimal reply.

Drawing Goeff into conflict was like wrestling quicksilver. No matter how he tried, MacGregor could not come to grips with this son. The boy forever slipped away.

"Not your game, Man of the House, is it Goeff?" asked MacGregor implying an unfavorable comparison with Gordie the younger brother understood.

"No Da," admitted Goeff, comfortable with his reply. "I don't like to fight."

"What!" MacGregor exploded to hear such heresy. "Not like to fight? And how else will you make your way in the world? You might as well say you don't want to be a man like your father!"

"I don't want to be a man like my father," Goeff repeated.

What was the boy saying? Trying to get a fix on Goeff's meaning, MacGregor looked closely at his son to make sure this was his son, a suspicion he had held before because the boy was so different from himself. And if he were not his father, who was? But Mary would refuse to encourage jealousy by answering the question, leaving MacGregor to subdue his own uncertainty as he did now. With a struggle. This was his son, but he was growing wrong. The man gave it one final try.

"How is a son who won't go up against his father to become a man?"

"Maybe I don't want to be a man," came the cold reply.

Staring in disbelief at this son who stood up to him by refusing to stand up to him, MacGregor felt frustration, then disgust.

"Oh, what's the use? This comes of too much mothering!" Abruptly he turned toward the car. "Tell your Ma I'll be back when I'm back," he growled. Slamming the door behind him and grinding the starter, MacGregor wheeled the car about and rattled down the road, each bump bruising his wounded spirits worse, reminding him of how he had been hurt. Here he was the Trout King and no one in his family even cared to know.

Certainly not Mary whose sole concern was keeping vigil over Gordie, breath for breath, so preoccupied with worry she neither heard her husband leave nor noticed Goeff pad softly in and out to check up on his brother.

Something was broken was the most that she could tell. Not physically, but broken all the same. In Gordie. Also in herself. Something broken, changed, or lost. She couldn't yet put together what it was. Couldn't separate Gordie's hurt from her own, although in sleep, if sleep it was, he did not appear in pain. Peaceful was how he looked. Peaceful and dazed. At rest, a smile sweetly flickering on and off his thickened lips. A smile she hadn't seen in years. Smile of the child before roughness replaced gentle play. Sweet and rough like his father, only – that was it. Mary identified her loss. Whatever sweetness she had cherished in MacGregor, the sweet inside of him, the secret side of him that she alone had known because she let him woo her with it when they loved, was gone.

And what was left? She shuddered at the answer, fear. Fear he would try to touch her again, to take her in the old familiar way. How could she bear the touch of him who had struck down her son? She couldn't. But how could she resist? And what would happen if she did? And if she let it happen, how would she feel? And which alternative was worse? A muddle of unhappy choices in a life where happiness was hard to find.

Weary with worry for her son and now for herself, Mary lightly touched his forehead with her fingers. It was not fevered. Then pressed her palm against his chest. Beneath the bellows of his breathing she could feel the steady pumping of his heart. All she could hope for at the moment. And a quiet night.

Covering him up she arose, to her surprise discovering Goeff staring from the other bed.

"Is Gordie going to be all right?" the boy whispered, lest noise disturb his brother.

"Yes," Mary lied, then told the truth, "He'll be his old self in the morning."

After tucking Goeff in and patting him good night, she felt her way along the unlit hall into her room, bumping against the doorway as she entered, clumsy with fatigue, collapsing fully dressed upon the covers, closing her eyes as she fell. Fast asleep, where MacGregor, groping for a light he could not find, stumbled upon her when he staggered in later that night, falling across her when he fell across the bed, cursing the dark for his inability to see, jarring her awake with fright.

To save herself, Mary tried to roll away but his weight was too heavy to escape.

"No!" she protested. "I can't. Leave me alone!"

Either MacGregor didn't hear or didn't want to hear. Two celebrations in one day had dulled all his senses but desire.

"Mary," he mumbled, remembering where he was and who she was and what he wanted.

"No!" she cried again. In vain.

Too insensate to hear her pleas and too aroused to heed her opposition, MacGregor sought her body for the satisfaction he desired. Perhaps if he had found the words that she found pleasing, she would have found a way to bear his touch without repugnance. But he was too impaired to communicate beyond the utterance of her name, and she was too appalled by him as father to allow him to act husband to herself.

"Mary!" he insisted once again, more urgently, more slurred, his tongue too thick and heavy for coherent speech, letting his hands express his wants language could not.

The harder she fought back the harder he became to overcome, as though he gathered strength from her resistance. It was no use. Mary knew it was no use. The only way to get away was to give him his way and get it over.

Beneath him MacGregor felt her body suddenly go limp and taking her submission as permission he gratified his need, while Mary turned her head to avoid his heavy breathing, breathing harder 'til he shuddered with release, rolling off her spent with pleasure into heavy sleep. To MacGregor this may have felt like love as usual, but to Mary it felt more like rape.

Wide away she lay beside him the remainder of the night numb with despair, her marriage torn beyond repair. While MacGregor slumbered unaware.

At breakfast time when she did not come out, Goeff looked in to see her looking blankly back at him without a greeting, without getting up.

"Gordie's still asleep," he announced, the message recalling Mary to responsibility.

She nodded comprehension.

"I'll have a look." Her tone of voice lacked feeling when she spoke, alerting Goeff to something strange about his mother, he did not know what.

When he was gone, Mary wrapped on a robe to cover up her body and hurried down the hall to insure recovery of her other son.

He lay as she had left him, curled up like an infant, infant sweet. Last night the sweetness was a comfort. It felt less assuring now. Vaguely disturbing. However, he was getting rest. Best to let him rest.

Wandering into the kitchen she did not recognize it for her own what with food left out to spoil and dishes soiled and unwashed. House proud she was, and did not tolerate dirt or disorder. But now, she did not care. What did it matter?

Filling a clean saucepan with water, leaving the faucet running, she pushed another pan off its burner, turned up the flame and waited for the boil. Something to drink was what she wanted. Pouring a cup, she watched the tea bag turn the water brown.

"I'll get my own to eat," Goeff declared seeing his mother in no mood to do for others, turning off the water she left on.

If she heard she did not signify, noticing of what she usually was not, unnoticing of what she usually observed. Clearing a place for herself at the table by pushing the offending plates away, she claimed the space that she had emptied for her own, sitting and sipping, sipping and thinking, thinking of not thinking, of not feeling, of relief.

Made anxious by changes in his world he could not fully fathom, Goeff quietly began restoring order to which he was accustomed by cleaning up around his mother.

"Where's breakfast?" None was waiting. It was MacGregor come to his aching senses and feeling worse for his arrival. What had he done to merit such neglect? Nothing he could recall.

"Well?" he asked again. "Am I to go to work without being fed?"

Mary did not even turn around.

"Feed yourself," she said, "Mr. MacGregor," using the title of respect to convey contempt.

"Say what?" he demanded. "Mr. MacGregor?" She had never called him by this epithet before and was never not to address him by it again.

Goeff marvelled at her ascendancy over MacGregor when the man was sober or mostly so. By comparison his mother was so small and yet his father, objecting all the while, yielded to her authority time and again. As he did now.

"Have it your way!" he snarled. "Ojay won't refuse me!" And he slammed out, hurt and bewildered by this undeserved mistreatment from his wife.

Only then did Goeff notice Gordie hanging back in the hallway door, tentatively peering in.

"Ma," called Goeff. "Here's Gordie!" glad to see his brother up and about.

This time Mary did turn around. It was indeed her older son.

"Gordie, come here," she demanded, wanting a closer look, the boy timidly coming forward, standing tensely for her inspection, acting hand-shy, cowering when she moved too suddenly.

"How do you feel?" she gently asked, softening in response to his new timidity.

"Fine," Gordie smiled to the extent his bruises would allow.

"You don't hurt?" Mary wanted to be sure.

"I don't hurt," Gordie wanting to give the answer she wanted to hear. Wanting to please. Not wanting to offend anyone. Ever again.

"Here's breakfast, Gordie. I made it special." Goeff sat his brother down and shared, leaving none for himself. It filled him up just watching Gordie eat.

Then both boys walked outside, the older following the younger, the younger now in charge, the younger seeming older, the older more a child.

Mary watched them in and out the remainder of the day, chatting with Gordie whenever he came through, receiving compliant replies, short and sweet and simple, confirming the alteration that she feared, fear for her son driving out any fear of husband. No more. Henceforth MacGregor would be made to keep his distance. Neither herself nor Goeff nor Gordie would be hurt again.

Armed with this resolution, Mary was ready for MacGregor when he returned that evening, confronting him as soon as he came through the door, her words and manner harsh and cold, communicating her displeasure before he could communicate his own.

"We've eaten," she declared. As much as saying she didn't want to eat with him. "There's food on the stove." Telling him to get it for himself. "Mr. MacGregor." Reasserting the formality she had now placed between them. Dutiful and dominant she was, giving him no right to complain nor room to object unless he wished to make her humor worse, which he did not.

Maybe it was her mood time of the month. Maybe that was it. Although MacGregor had never seen her this surly, so ominously dark. Ah well, no doubt the storm would soon blow over. 'Til then he'd stay out of harm's way.

Setting his place with a dish and glass he had to wash, he filled his plate and, sitting down, began to eat, chewing slowly, thoughtfully, in silence, wishing she'd get over what was wrong, wondering what it was this time. Probably the little tussle with Gordie last night. But that was done. Why couldn't the woman just forgive and move on? Himself, he didn't put much stock in memory. Didn't remember much of what she swore he did. They never could agree over the past. While he let bygones go, she would bring up what he was wanting to forget, refuse to leave bad enough alone. She couldn't understand life was too short to lead it looking back. Bury the bad and hope for the better. His way.

But none of this deliberation did he dare share with Mary. Since she was simmering already, why bring her to a boil? Time would cool her anger off. Meanwhile, he would go and quench his thirst for male companionship no woman could provide nor truly understand. For comraderie. Mary, she thought it was for drinking, but she was wrong. The drinking like the joking and the sparring back and forth with words were all one, ways for men to feel like men with other men. Later, when he returned, they could satisfy the longing for which he and she had married. He would speak sweetly and she would soften to his words. And afterwards they would talk about whatever displeasure he had caused. Then he could tell his news and she would want to know. Later.

Now, she gave him no farewell because she wished him none. Dismissed him, she did, and he departed in no better grace than when he came.

Out front the boys were piecing parts of the broken generator into one another, Goeff directing his brother how to lift and fit the heavy rotor.

"On your feet as good as new!" MacGregor greeted Gordie, cheered by the sight of his older son now back in working order.

Gordie retreated a few steps while Goeff spoke up to cover for his brother.

"He's giving me good help. We're learning how it works from taking it apart and piecing it back together." This was an exercise through which the father frequently had taught his sons.

Used to communicating through the older to the younger, MacGregor did not know what to make of this reversal, Gordie so reticent and Goeff so bold. Confusing to have them change like this. Too confusing to sort out right now.

"Keep trying," the man encouraged. "If you can't get it right today, I'll give you a hand tomorrow."

Surprised by the leniency of his father's response, Goeff kept his brother at it for another hour and then led him into the house where Mary was slumped at the kitchen table surrounded by the litter of the evening meal, nothing cleaned up or put away.

"We're going to bed, Ma," Goeff announced, concealing the unease he felt.

"Are you tired?" Mary asked, ignoring Goeff for Gordie.

"I don't mind," Gordie vaguely smiled, agreeable to what she said.

"All right then," she replied. "Give us a hug." And each boy hugged his mother, Goeff hugging back, Gordie willing to be hugged, Mary sensitive to the difference. Mary worried. Mary by herself. Feeling so alone. Wishing she could go to sleep as well. Too troubled in her mind to shut the suffering off. Denied the simple mercy of unconscious rest. Praying for deliverance from waking pain. If not deliverance, at least relief. Desperate for relief. At last seeking solace where she had seen her husband find it, but finding it in secret so nobody would know. Her prayers gradually answered. Blessed sleep.

Not where MacGregor expected to find her, Mary fallen forward on the kitchen table, head cradled on her arms, snoring softly. He nudged her gently. No response. Then he tried to slowly pull her up but she exploded into a rage of profanity and a snarl of hate he had never heard before, flailing at him with her arms until he lowered her down and she fell forward back to sleep as he had found her.

What was this? He stood a long time wondering what to do, finally concluding there was nothing he could do. Turning toward the bedroom he almost upended as a bottle slipped like a bar of soap beneath his foot and skidded into several empty others on the floor. What was this? He looked carefully around. Something told him he had better watch his step.

CHAPTER TWELVE

THE COWBOY'S ADVICE

Several days had passed since Front revealed the great trout to Sam, time during which the man mulled over how his son might angle for the fish. He himself had no experience with a trout so large in a place so difficult. Only after casting back and forth through many memories did he finally catch hold of an idea that had the feel of a definite, albeit slight, possibility. He smiled at the recollection. Why he loved fishing, for the stories which went with it. To tell the idea, he would have to tell the story.

"Come sit with me outside," Sam invited Front after dinner. "Men talk," he explained to Estelle who understood they each had different ways of being with their son.

"This is a long road to making a suggestion," Sam began as Front settled back to listen, "but I want to share with you an idea given me by a character who claimed it worked for a very large trout only. Swore it worked for him and I don't doubt his word. Of all people he was an actual cowboy whom I met by chance one summer before you were born. I was out fishing one of those great western rivers where lunkers of the variety you've discovered are more common then they are here. Although I've never heard of any the size of this beast."

His father had a way of spinning yarns that Front found captivating.

"Rivers out there," Sam continued, "are much larger than our eastern streams. More deeply powerful and much more treacherous to wade. The holes are hidden by the turbulence and can down a man who isn't careful, like they did me. Fifty yards downstream I was before I knew what happened. Ass over teakettle, more underwater than above, lucky for me I didn't lose my gear and get drowned in the bargain. I would have too, if the Good Lord, as He always seems to do when I fall in, wasn't watching over me. So instead getting dunked for good, I fetched up a wetter and wiser man on some shallows He held out for fishermen like me who don't have sense enough to pay attention where they're stepping.

"So there I was, soaked to the skin, sitting waist deep in stupidity, and looking up I see this tall fella on the bank leaning against his horse, both of them looking at me, the guy rolling a cigarette as untroubled as could be. 'Need some help?' he asked when he was done. 'Hell no!' I replied. 'I don't need any help. Not now. Of course a minute ago my need was considerably different. But I guess you saw that.'

"'I did,' he admitted, cool as you please. 'Well,' I answered getting hot, 'is it your idea of sport out in this friendly part of the world to let strangers kill themselves losing their footing in these death traps you call rivers?' I felt like blaming him.

"'Not my idea at all,' he says. 'Thought maybe it was yours.' Then he grinned. And for the life of me I couldn't help it. I burst out laughing. No doubt about it, I was a sorry sight to behold with no one to thank but myself.

"To do him credit he waded in and gave me a hand up, helping me to shore because to tell the truth my legs were pretty shaky which he could see but had the good grace to ignore. Then he sat me against a tree and rolled another cigarette while I was watching and getting myself back together.

"'How do you do that?' I asked. 'Using only one hand?' It was quite a trick. 'Practice, I suppose,' he answered. 'Never really thought about it.' And I don't think he ever had. 'With that kind of skill,' I suggested, 'you ought to try tying flies.' 'Oh I've done some of that too,' he drawled, 'though we use bigger ones out here than those little critters drying on your vest. Course I can't tie a fly with one hand, but I can come pretty close. I can do it with two.'

"'No cleverness in that,' I told him. 'So can I. And as no doubt you've noticed, clumsiness is one of my strong suits.' He cocked his head like he was sizing up a prospect. 'But can you do it while holding the hook between the fingers of one hand?' he asked. Well I wasn't going to let him play me for a fool. 'Certainly not,' I called his bluff. 'I use a vise to hold the hook like every other fly tier in this world. And so do you. Just because I fell in your river doesn't mean I'm going to fall for anything. Tying flies happens to be a subject I know something about!'

"Well he looks at me like he was looking me over, and to this day I'm grateful not to be a betting man because I would have wagered what little I had on what, it turned out, was how little I knew. An expert's knowledge and experience can create a lot of pride and vanity – the stuff born suckers are made of. Happily for me this guy didn't tempt me with an offer because sure as sin I would have bitten and bitten deep. Instead, he just smiled that slow smile of his and said 'Here, I'll show you something you can take back East with you.'

"Then he strolls over to his horse and rummages around in one of his saddle bags, returning with a hook, some thread, a bit of floss, a couple feathers, some animal hair (I couldn't make out what kind). all the ingredients of a fly right there in the palm of his hand. A hard hand it was, tough with callouses and stained with dirt.

"'You want me to hold the hook?' I offered, not wanting to see the man embarrass himself for he had treated me kindly in his way. 'No', he declined. 'You might enjoy watching though.' And with that he proceeded, with the assistance of his teeth to anchor the thread from time to time, to tie up a fly as pretty as you please. I couldn't believe it. Darnedest exhibition of manual dexterity I ever saw, and I told him so.

"'Only takes two fingers to hold the hook,' he explained, 'so that leaves three with nothing to do plus five to spare on the other hand. How many fingers does it take an Easterner to tie a fly with anyway?' He was gigging me for being a tenderfoot, but he was right. He knew a whole lot more about living in his world than I did. So I just laughed. Told him he had shown me a demonstration I would certainly remember, though probably never attempt to imitate. He chuckled and gave me the fly which I've still got stashed in one tackle box or another. Then we fell to talking about how to fish the river.

"That's when he shared this idea. I had asked about what time of day was best and he replied he didn't know since he only fished late at night. Well, this was new to me. Day fishing such a torrent was hazardous enough without complicating the job with darkness, and I told him so.

"'Actually night isn't as dark as you think', he disagreed, 'particularly when you're by a river. Under a clear sky, running water collects moonlight like a mirror. Lived in the city so long you've lost use of your natural senses, that's all. Give your eyes two or three hours to adjust and you'll begin to see like an animal.'

"But I was unpersuaded. 'You don't mean to tell me you can spot a rise in the dark?' He shook his head. 'Don't have to. At night you don't cast to the fish, you make them come to you. Tie on the biggest fly you've got and junk it out there. It will scare the small trout off, but not the big ones. They'll be interested. Figure it might be something with size enough worth eating. Big trout feel safer feeding in the dark. They act less cautious. Don't see as well and sure don't fight as smart. Do stupid things at night they'd never do come daylight. Even had one beach itself trying to get away. If you're around the next few days, I'll take you out one night and show you what it's like.' But I claimed I was leaving soon and didn't have the time.

"Kicked myself ever since for not taking up his invitation. Felt like I was risking enough wading in daylight without upping the ante by doing it at night. Also, I had visions of stepping on a rattlesnake or bumping into a range bull which were of no concern to him, I'm sure, but worried my imagination something fearful. So I've carried his idea around untested all these years. Maybe now's the time to try it out. You could cast something splashy into that pool late at night and, who knows, you might stir up some action."

Fly fishing for the great trout at night! Front had never thought of that, while the image of the Cowboy caught his fancy -- rising to the challenge of facing down an enemy alone. Except he didn't want to do it all alone.

"Will you come with me?" he asked his father.

"Count on it," answered Sam. "I can't imagine any animals in this part of the world I'd fear running up against at night. Of course there is your mother to consider, what she'll say. Although I guess she won't think we're any crazier about fishing than she already does."

Front smiled sadly. The joke was funny and it was not. His mother's disapproval was true, but so was her support. Another painful contradiction in his family. Like his parents being close to him and distant from each other. Fishing itself made mixed, but not this expedition. He felt eager.

"I can bring my flashlight so we don't get lost," Front suggested, starting to formulate his plans.

"Yes, that would make traveling easier. But I don't think the Cowboy would favor the easy way. He didn't have much use for artificial light. Unless you've got strong feelings to the contrary, I believe we should follow his example, use cover of darkness to keep out of sight and train our eyes to see as best we can."

Front thought about the Cowboy, this storied fisherman from his father's past and could not resist the call of his advice. Agreed. They would wait for the moon to reach its brightest shine. Meanwhile, he had work to do. The pool must be reconnoitered to determine how to get a clear cast, where on the bank he must stand, how to reach the spot raising minimal alarm. He had never fished like this before. Mounting a campaign. Mapping out strategy. Knowing the particular quarry he was after. The whole process thrilled him as if he was committing an enormous dare, although what it was, other than failure or falling in, he could not imagine. But he mentioned the feeling to his father and was surprised by the seriousness of the man's response.

"Yes. I've been worrying about that too. Quite a risk you'll be taking."

"What risk?" Front was used to his mother worrying, not his father. "At worst nothing may happen. At best I may catch the fish to end all fishing."

"Yes. That's the risk I was thinking of. Maybe the one you are sensing."

Front shook his head. "You've caught big trout before. You have this summer. And you were happy when you did. Hungry for more. Why shouldn't I be the same?"

"Because," explained Sam, his voice softening, "this is not just a big trout you're after. This is different. Stop and think. This fish is probably older than you in human years. While in the time used to measure the life span of its species it's among the eldest and largest of its kind. Who knows? Perhaps there never has been or ever will be its like again. It's a big responsibility to kill one of nature's grandest creations. You know me, I'm not usually like your mother about this, reluctant to exploit other creatures for the sake of sport. But this one you've discovered, in my wildest dreams, and I have dreamed of big trout all my life, I never conjured up such a fish."

"Are you telling me not to try?"

"No. Only to make this choice carefully. Sometimes great ambitions have unexpected outcomes. That's all I mean."

"If you were me, what would you do?"

"I can't answer that," Sam replied, "because I'm not you. I'm older and grown more cautious. But if you mean speaking for who I am today, no. No, I don't think I would try to catch such a fish."

The boy considered his father's words, weighing their vague but compelling warning. Then he waited for his feelings to decide. First there was a twinge of fear followed by a rush of excitement he could not resist.

"I want to try!" he exclaimed.

"So be it!" pronounced Sam. "We've had some great times fishing, you and I, but I have a feeling this trip is going to be the humdinger to top them all! Now, let me check your line, put on a fresh leader and make sure of all the knots. No sense not doing this up right. What fly do you want to use? You could tie up a whopping big parachute since that seems to be your favorite.”

Front turned the idea over then threw it out.

“No,” he declared. Then his face lit up. “I want to use one of yours.”

Sam was surprised.

“Sure. Which one?”

“One of the ones on your hat.”

“An Outrageous Fly?” Sam was delighted.

“The red and blue.” Front had already made his choice.

“The Desperation Special?” Sam hooted with laughter. “Well why not!” And they both came laughing back into the house, Estelle excluded from the joke but happy they were happy. Whatever disaffection cooled the marriage, she loved Sam’s way of fathering their son. Men!

Glancing up from her book, Estelle made a bid for Front’s attention.

“Ready for bed? I’ll read to you if you like.” Her timing was correct.

“OK,” Front yawned. He was tired from excitement. Too tired for tying flies, not tired enough to go to sleep. Not yet.

The opening for which his mother daily waited when she could catch her active son run out of energy, unoccupied, accessible to what she loved to share. Myths, fairy tales, and legends were her selection, subtly feeding his imagination without him knowing he was being fed. To Front it felt like being lulled with speech, drowsing, drifting in and out, skipping words, missing passages, at last losing touch with voice itself, sinking beneath awareness into sleep. Burying the stories deep.

Turning out her son's light, Estelle passed Sam on the way to bed.

"Good night," he called down the hall.

"Good night," she echoed back across the emptiness between them.

Next morning Sam departed early before the other two had awakened. He had not slept well. The giant fish swam through his dreams troubling his rest with images he neither understood nor liked. In one, Front rode astride the trout. In another, the fish was leading the river on a rampage.

Estelle, perhaps because she was a teacher, believed in the telling power of dreams; but Sam did not credit them with meaning. When they disturbed his sleep as they did now, his immediate concern was to remedy fatigue and restore well being. A good hot breakfast, that was the cure. And good conversation. Ojay's, on the off chance she'd be open early. At least worth a try. And he was glad when, from a distance down the highway, he saw the light through her window beaming bright. She was already serving customers. One customer. He recognized the car when he pulled up. MacGregor's. She drinking coffee while the big man ate.

"Hello! Hello!" greeted Sam. "Anything left to eat or has MacGregor cleaned you out?" This to Ojay.

"There's still a scrap or two if you ain't fussy," Ojay replied getting up and going back to work. "Off to the west branch again Sam?"

"No. You and the Reverend and MacGregor here have me convinced. Big trout lay close to home."

"Not anymore," spoke up MacGregor, mopping the last of the egg off his plate with a piece of toast. "Between us, we've taken the best Grisham's Well has to offer. And they don't grow bigger nowhere else."

"Are you sure?" retorted Sam, irritated by MacGregor's complacency. "Secrets are what fishing is about. Only the river knows them all. You've caught a big brown, Mac, no argument there. But you know what they say about records being made to be broken."

"You sound like you're sitting on a secret yourself," answered MacGregor sensing danger, in no mood for more to go wrong than already had.

"Maybe I am and maybe I'm not," teased Sam. He couldn't resist volunteering more than he promised Front he would reveal. Too much.

Now Ojay caught the drift of what he wasn't saying.

"So you've found a bigger fish, Sam?" she asked as she delivered him his meal, carrying the hint to its conclusion.

Sam shut himself up by eating while the others watched. It was one of his strengths and failings and he knew it. He loved provoking competition. He throve on it at work. As the man to beat, he egged on other salesmen to do their best to catch him causing him to do his best to win. But this was not the time or place. If he hadn't been so tired. He blamed his indiscretion on fatigue, then noticed how MacGregor did not look well slept himself. Maybe he could change the subject. So, innocent of the reversals in MacGregor's family life, he teased the conversation in a new direction.

"Your wife not feeding you breakfast anymore, Mac? Has it come to this?"

MacGregor flushed with rage at the hurt Sam's joke unknowingly inflicted.

"If mine's let me go hungry, so has yours!" he exploded. "As for my record, it won't be broken by the likes of you!" and standing up MacGregor threw his napkin down upon the table and stormed out, Ojay as surprised by this abrupt departure as Sam.

"I must have caught him on a raw day," observed Sam. "Wonder why?"

Ojay wondered too. Yesterday was Wednesday and no Mary. And here's MacGregor showing up unfed five mornings in a row. While he was not a confidant like Mary, he was nonetheless a friend. What she liked about Bishop's Place. Small enough so there was little social choice. You took folks as you found them, shortcomings and all. No changing to suit others or keep up. The same way they took you. Doing for each other like a family. Was Mary needing to be done for now? Then there was Sam's broadside at MacGregor.

"Have you found a fish to take the title?" she asked.

"Would I tell him if I had?" laughed Sam trying to discount the truth which he had told, hoping she would see it as an idle boast.

"I don't know. I don't think so. I guess not," Ojay finally concluded. "But he took you at your word. You've got him worried if that was what you wanted. He'll have his eye on you from here on out."

Not what Sam wanted, but too late now.

CHAPTER THIRTEEN

THE REVEREND GETS TO HAVE HIS SAY

"You're dreary company today, MacGregor," complained the Reverend about his brooding friend as the two walked silently along the river seeking open water where one could cast down from above while the other worked up from below. What had begun as an accidental meeting of two loners years ago had become an afternoon companionship both men looked forward to several times a week.

Although the Reverend had preceded MacGregor to Bishop's Place a full five years, both men were still considered more naturalized than native by those founding families, like the Detmers, who could trace their lineage back over generations to the encampment from which the town originally had grown. Both men were accepted, but not entirely. 'Once a newcomer, always an outsider', as MacGregor once bitterly complained to his friend.

In fact, it was this shared exclusion from the community in which they lived that first brought the men together, then a compatibility based on envy each had for the other, arousing that hostility through which their friendship was commonly expressed. Envy based on admiration although neither would admit it. Bound by rules he represented, the Reverend wished he had MacGregor's outlaw freedom; while MacGregor wished he did not annually have to earn respect the other man's position guaranteed.

"Is it attending church this Sunday that has soured you so?" the Reverend wanted to know.

"You're the least of my problems, whatever you'll have to say."

"Do you want to tell me? Or would you rather keep your troubles to yourself?"

"I'd rather have no troubles at all!" MacGregor was exasperated by the question. As though he had a lot of choice. "It's Mary. She's not herself. I don't know why."

Like Ojay, the Reverend had missed his Wednesday visit with Mary, a bright spot in his week. She would look in on him like she was looking after him and he liked that. Often she would bring him something special she had baked, a gift of caring. Part of her self-appointed duty to the church, ministering to its minister.

"Have you asked her what is wrong? Have you made up to her?"

MacGregor's exasperation turned to disgust at his friend's incapacity to understand.

"She's too sullen to be spoken to and in no temper to be touched."

This did not sound like the Mary whom the Reverend knew. Something was wrong all right. Better to cheer his friend by changing topics.

"Well at least you're Trout King for another year."

MacGregor frowned.

"Maybe so and maybe not. Sam Henry's on to one that's got mine beat."

"He told you so?"

"Worse. He didn't mean to, but the truth slipped out. If he had told me outright, I wouldn't have believed him."

Now the Reverend had nothing to say. No comfort to offer. So he busied himself selecting a fly while MacGregor did the same, each man discouraged from further talk as they fished together until dusk closed down the day. Then they went their separate ways. The Reverend to work on his sermon, MacGregor to face what awaited him at home.

What awaited him at home? MacGregor hoped for better than he feared. Cautiously he climbed the steps, attempting to sneak past her irritation. Furtively he pushed open the door.

"Mr. MacGregor!" she snapped and once again he felt the bite of her reproof. "Food's cold. Heat it or not as you like."

The place was unkempt and so was she, defiant of caring about appearances, daring him to complain which he did not.

"The Reverend asked about you," MacGregor offered in peace. Perhaps someone beside himself could draw her out and do it softly. But no such luck. She was not interested. Did not respond.

He looked around for the boys but they were not in evidence. She had warned them out of sight 'til he was driven off for the evening. No chances. Mary was taking no chances. She was giving him no quarter.

Condemned to eat alone in silence once again, MacGregor grew hungry for companionship elsewhere.

"I'll be going," he announced when he was done. She did not object as he crept away.

Watching him leave, Mary was grateful and regretful to be left alone. Night was the worst. Sorrow was overwhelming. She had to quell her pain if she would get to sleep. But first she had to get her sons to bed.

Having heard the rattle of their father's car departing, the boys walked in from where they had been staying quiet, Goeff with his arm protectively around his older brother, Gordie reliant on the other's care, both grown inseparably close. Sweet to see until Mary considered the cause, wishing she could obliterate the memory of that and what came after. Unable to forget.

Without being instructed, Goeff began to wash and put away what his mother was too tired to straighten up. Gordie helped as he was told. While Mary let them clean if that was what they wanted. She didn't care. They were her only care.

"Sweet dreams," she wished them each, kissing them both good night. Wishing the same for herself, having little faith in wishes, reaching for what worked better. If only she had friends to talk to who would understand. But who would understand? Some wrongs there are too shameful to be shared, sins better kept concealed from a disapproving world.

After all, what would Cora say if Cora knew? Even Ojay, less quick to judge than Cora, less likely to condemn, would still be sure to take the woman's part against MacGregor and by blaming him blame family and herself for what occurred. As for the Reverend, he was MacGregor's friend more than her own. Then there was reputation to consider. What would people think? Standing, so hard to earn in Bishop's Place, could be so easily destroyed.

No. Secrecy must keep the shame from being known. If this meant keeping distant from her friends, she'd do without her Wednesdays for a while. Just for a while, she told herself, while she gathered strength to put up a pretense, to act like all was well when it was not. 'Til then she would struggle on alone, helping herself as best she could. Like this. There. Already it was working. She felt dulled and numbed and drowsy. One more dose and sleep would take her. And it did. She didn't even hear the bottle hit the floor. Nor did she see her younger son come pick it up, stare at her for a moment, then switch off the kitchen light and silently return to bed.

Meanwhile, as Mary slept into oblivion and MacGregor found refuge trading boasts and arguing with cronies at the Tavern, the Reverend was deep in study over what to say on Sunday. No simple sermon, this. But a bargain he had made in anger that he must keep without degenerating into diatribe. He must address the failing of his friend without attacking him. And Mary. He must consider her. What he preached against the husband would be charged against the wife, so he must speak to all, not just to one. Besides, failings were not the measure of a man, thank God. For if they were than everyone was lost. Failings were the gift of imperfection, that and adversity the challenges that human kind were meant to struggle to accept and strive to overcome.

He felt relieved. There it was, the message he was meant to give. As usual, the search was sure if he would let his thoughts get lost in wandering. If he would only trust and let them go, sooner or later they would return with the idea he wanted that he did not know he wanted until they found it for him. From reflection came discovery. He felt grateful, and giving thanks picked up his yellow pad and pencil to begin composing what he had to say.

Still hard to do knowing MacGregor would take offense in any case. On numerous occasions the man had preached against sermons, accusing the Reverend of superiority by talking down to those he held himself above.

"Have you ever actually heard a sermon, MacGregor?" the Reverend would ask, and his friend would stiffen at the question, insulted by the thought.

"I have not! What do you think I am, a fool? If I know a thing is poison, I don't take it to find out!"

No arguing with prejudice, and so the Reverend let the charges stand, giving up on getting him to church until the luck at Grisham's Well when casting for a fish created opportunity to catch MacGregor. Striking hard, the Reverend's bargain was unfairly made as he well knew, his terms or none at all. A poor offer at a bad time with worse to follow if it were refused. What other choice did MacGregor have?

Too honest to deny trapping his friend into attendance by extortion of the moment, the Reverend hoped an honorable end would justify dishonorable means. If he could cause MacGregor to soberly reflect upon the failing of his ways then perhaps some good could be accomplished. If not, the story and its moral was a worthy one to hear, which none would hear unless he buckled down to work. Thinking was the easy part. Wrestling with words to pin expression down was what was hard. Time was a wasting. Sunday would be here soon enough and sure enough it was, the final touches on his sermon finished as the early bells began to toll, rushing him to church to arrive before his congregation.

Not the only person in a hurry.

"Come along or we'll be late," Mary urged the boys. "Goeff, finish helping Gordie dress. I'll start the car."

"No need," MacGregor interrupted. "I'll do the driving."

"What? You to church?" His surprise announcement caused her to breach formality she meant to keep.

"Why not? Do I need a ticket or a reservation? Is it some private club from which I'm barred?" Sarcasm to cover his discomfort.

"It's free for all Mr. MacGregor," Mary replied, restoring her ascendancy. "Only you've never come before. Why now?"

"I'm expected. The Reverend took my word. I mean to go and make it good to get it back." MacGregor hated having to explain.

Mary could not imagine how the Reverend had extracted such a promise, nor why MacGregor felt obliged to keep it. Then she noticed what her husband wore. Clean trousers and a buttoned shirt, stuffed into the jacket he was married in, the only one he had. He looked done up for some comical occasion except she was past seeing humor in the man.

They arrived in time to join the crowd of everybody else, Cora on the watch, approaching them to speak, dispensing with frivolity, getting to the point.

"Mary, you don't look well. Were you home sick on Wednesday?"

Better to feign an illness than to tell the truth, so Mary lied.

"I was. But I'm feeling better now."

"You don't look better," Cora disagreed, Mary's appearance contradicting what she said. Then with customary lack of tact, Cora acknowledged the unusual presence of MacGregor.

"What brings you to church?" Her question was invasive of his privacy.

It did not please MacGregor to have to answer for his actions to anyone, particularly to Cora, Mary's long time sympathizer whose support he knew was partly founded on dislike of him.

"I'm here because I'm here," deliberately giving her the satisfaction of no answer at all. None of her business, and Cora get the message, filing it away with other instances consistent with her low opinion of the man. He was as sociable as a distempered dog.

Now if she was Mary, MacGregor would be brought to heel. But she was not, and besides there were the boys to consider, so she spoke to them, or thought she did. Acutally she spoke at them, to Gordie in deference of his being older.

"Been behaving yourselves, I hope for the sake of your mother?"

Gordie just smiled back. What was the matter with the boy? Had he lost his sense? But Goeff quickly replied.

"Yes mum. We're doing what she tells us," saying what she wanted to hear so she'd leave them alone.

Now organ music called them in, Cora and Wally following Mr.and Mrs. Detmer down the aisle to sit in the front pew that unofficially belonged to them befitting their position. Other families seating themselves according to the informal rule of local prominence, nearness to the front for those with the longest history in town. Mary and the boys seated themselves further back with MacGregor who was fortunately ignorant of the social difference seating made.

As the Reverend mounted to the pulpit and the service began, MacGregor prepared to pass the time with his mind elsewhere which he did until the first hymn when everybody rose to standing and so did he. When everybody sang and he did not, withholding his participation in silent protest at attending. Then he heard it. From among the multitude of voices there came one that wounded him with recollection and with loss, the voice beside him. Mary's. He had forgotten how she used to sing when they were early married. How the beauty of his wife was expressed in song.

Too soon the music over and everyone sat down. Words were spoken. Words were read. A plate was passed. Then they arose once more. He hoped they would, for now he longed to hear her sing again, and when she did more memories were stirred, more longing felt. Why couldn't they keep singing and forget the talk? But no such luck. Now the Reverend's time to speak had come. And MacGregor's time to listen.

While the congregation settled back to hear their minister, the Reverend silently surveyed the faces he had come to know so well. The same old faces he was used to seeing every Sunday, except for one. He waited 'til he caught MacGregor's eyes, nodded ever so slightly, and commenced to preach.

"The problem with us human beings, as the Bible teaches, is that we can't leave well enough alone. Given much we want more. Given good we want bad. Given warning we are tempted. Given temptation we succumb. The truth is, human kind went downhill from the first. And we've never managed to climb back to where we started.

"'In the beginning' we are told, 'God created the heaven and the earth.' Notice the order of Creation if you will. God's priorities. First form from void, then light from darkness, sky from water, land from sea, plant from earth, sun and moon, birds and fish, creatures of the land, and last of all, not first, man himself. Worth remembering, because we often act like we're the most important part of God's creation and we're not. Only the most troublesome.

"'And the Lord God took the man, and put him into the Garden of Eden to dress it and keep it. And the Lord God commanded the man saying, of every tree of the garden thou mayest freely eat, but of the tree of knowledge of good and evil, thou shalt not eat of it, for in the day thou eatest thereof, thou shalt surely die.' And with this one condition God gave man the power of choice.

"God's word plainly spoken and clearly understood, yet man and woman chose instead to believe a serpent's lie, 'ye shall not surely die.' And to be enticed by the serpent's promise, 'ye shall be as gods, knowing good and evil.' A lie and a promise were all it took to deny the truth of what they knew and to yearn for more abundance than already had been given.

"And what did getting what they wanted get Adam and Eve? For the momentary satisfaction of desire and ambition, they gave up everlasting life. Becoming wise with knowledge they became ashamed about themselves, hid from sight when God called, and were driven out of Eden for their disobedience, condemned to a life of struggle and an end of death. And all of this was only the beginning. There was worse to come."

Shifting uneasily in his seat, MacGregor did not find being preached at to his liking. It was too one-sided. He felt trapped. Here the Reverend was freely holding forth, while he himself must sit in silence and endure. No stopping his friend now.

"Adam and Eve, they had a family. Two sons, Cain and Abel, both eager to please the Lord, bringing the best to him each had to offer. Abel succeeding in the eyes of the Lord while Cain did not.

"'And Cain was very wroth, and his countenance fell.' Downcast that his best did not find favor, was not deemed good enough, in a fit of jealous rage 'Cain rose up against Abel his brother and slew him.' Then when the Lord asked the whereabouts of Abel, Cain denied any knowledge of the murder, 'and he said, I know not. Am I my brother's keeper?'

"And so we come to brother killing brother. Despite knowing good from evil, man chooses evil over good, then covers up the crime he committed with a lie. But the Lord was not fooled by a lie. He never is. And Cain was driven further out from Eden. One generation removed from the Garden and look what mankind had already accomplished: anger, envy, violence, and deceit. But there was worse to come."

For MacGregor, it was feeling worse already. He was wondering if the bargain for his fish was worth the aggravation he was undergoing now. Well, let the Reverend have his say. He couldn't talk forever.

"Then the generations of Adam and Eve began to populate the earth, and as they multiplied so did mankind's capacity for doing wrong until, we are told 'God saw the wickedness of man was great in the earth, and that every imagination of the thoughts of his heart was only evil continually. And it repented the Lord that he had made man on earth, and it grieved him and his heart. And the Lord said, I will destroy man whom I have created from the face of the earth.' Notice God didn't say he would 'reform' man. He said 'destroy'. Because He had no reforming power. You see, God gave up control of his creations when he gave human beings choice, while given choice, human beings lost their capacity for perfect good.

"'And God looked upon the earth, and, behold, it was corrupt; for all flesh had corrupted his way upon the earth.' Oh this was a perilous time! There was the earth mired in human wickedness and there was God poised to eliminate corruption by eliminating man. Which brings us to Noah." And the Reverend gazed in the direction of MacGregor who gazed defiantly back at him.

"God must have paused for a moment for a final look at those he was about to destroy because it was then He noticed Noah; 'a just man and perfect in his generations.' And Noah 'found grace in the eyes of the Lord,' because God saw hope in Noah, the hope of a new beginning. And we, you and I, found grace through Noah because God would have killed the lot of us right then and there were it not for this one upright man and his family.

"So God relented, you know the story, and commanded Noah to build an ark, taking into it his household and pairs of all the living creatures of God's creation to ride out the flood in safety and replenish the earth when it was over. Which is what happened. 'And Noah only remained alive, and they that were with him in the ark.' Now God and man could build anew, evil which went before having been washed away. Except they had to begin from where they were, not where Creation started.

"The earth wasn't Eden anymore, and the generations since Adam and Eve had changed God's view of man. 'And the Lord said in his heart, I will not again curse the ground for man's sake; for the imagination of man's heart is evil from his youth; neither will I again smite any more every living thing, as I have done.' God saw man's human nature for the evil it possessed and he made a covenant with Noah, a promise; there would be no more floods. Man's imperfect nature was his to manage, while the destruction of man was to be left to man alone. 'Who so sheddeth man's blood, by man shall his blood be shed.' Not by God.

"So Noah was allowed to start over. 'And God blessed Noah and his sons and said unto them, Be fruitful and multiply and replenish the earth.' And Noah did his best which was very good because, remember, Noah was as good a man as God could find. However, upright though he was, Noah was only human – imperfect in his nature and capable of wrongful choice. As we are shown."

Here the Reverend paused and in the silence MacGregor could feel the point of all this preaching coming, although what the lesson was he did not know.

" 'And the sons of Noah, that went forth from the ark, were Shem and Ham and Japheth: and Ham the father of Canaan. These are the three sons of Noah: and of them was the whole earth overspread. And Noah began to be a husbandman.' He began to farm. 'And he planted a vineyard; and he drank of the wine, and was drunken; and he was uncovered within his tent.'

"There lay Noah, drunk. Naked in his drunkeness. Asleep. So what was to be done? Should anything be done? Then 'Ham the father of Canaan saw the nakedness of his father and told his two bretheren without. And Shem and Japheth took a garment and laid it upon their shoulders, and went backward, and covered the nakedness of their father; and their faces were backward, and they saw not their father's nakedness.' Why not? Why did they not want to see Noah's nakedness? To spare his shame? To spare themselves? We are not told. All we know is that they covered up their father's frailty and chose not to look at what was plainly to be seen.

"As for Ham, what did he gain from informing on his father? 'And Noah awoke from his wine, and he knew what his younger son had done unto him. And he said, Cursed be Canaan; a servant of servants shall he be unto his bretheren. And he said, Blessed be the Lord God of Shem; and Canaan shall be his servant. God shall enlarge Japheth, and he shall dwell in the tents of Shem; and Canaan shall be his servant.'

"What happened to the son who looked and told? Noah blessed and rewarded the two who denied the truth and cursed and punished the one who saw and spoke it. Why? To protect his own frailty.

"Frailty. That's what being human is about. From the beginning our nature has been flawed. Perhaps Noah's frailty was drink. What is yours? What is mine? What do we want kept secret? What do we want left alone? What failings do we protect at the expense of those we love? And when they point our failings out to us do we lie, deny, and punish our accusers? Or do we listen, recognize ourselves, and strive to overcome? Overcoming, that's what being human is about. Accepting and addressing our imperfections. Not being perfect. We lost our chance for choosing that when we left Eden.

"As for our duty to the ones we love, do we like Shem and Japheth avert our eyes and cover up the truth for fear the loved one will react unlovingly if truth be told? Or are we willing to make Ham's choice? To gaze with open eyes upon the truth, to speak it honestly, and to accept whatever angry consequences may occur?

"And what is this truth that we should be so protective and act so afraid? Frailty in all its human forms. Each of us has our share. Even the Noahs among us are flawed, because as good a man as Noah was, he was only human. 'And Noah lived after the flood three hundred and fifty years. And all the days of Noah were nine hundred and fifty years, and he died.' Let us pray."

"Thank God that's over," muttered MacGregor to himself, grateful he had paid his due and was freed from further obligation. Yet, as he stood up with the congregation for the final hymn, he felt a wave of sadness. This was the last time to hear his wife in song. And as he did, he ached with torment for forgiveness that would yield her to him. So close they stood and yet so far apart.

The crowd was slow in filing out as many stopped to thank the Reverend at the door before departing. Impatiently MacGregor waited for his turn. Not because he wanted to thank the Reverend himself. Just to be free to leave.

At last he was. Each man eyed the other, speechless, half amused. Neither had seen the other in official garb before – MacGregor in a jacket, the Reverend in a gown. Each felt awkward on account of dress. Finally the Reverend spoke.

"Well, Mac. What did you think of the sermon?"

Because MacGregor was preoccupied with other thoughts, he was slower than usual to fire back.

"I think Noah was right!"

The Reverend didn't understand.

"How so?"

Briefly MacGregor warmed to his conclusion.

"A man's drinking is his own business. As for those who interfere, they deserve whatever punishment they get!"

The Reverend was unsurprised. He had expected some objection. Besides, MacGregor seemed chastened as well. Sobered by the sermon, the Reverend wondered?

No. By something else. It was not words from the pulpit that had subdued MacGregor, but Mary's spirit singing by his side. Her voice was just as pure and uplifting as he remembered when they were courting. How it had charmed him then was how it charmed him now. When did she stop? Why did she stop? She didn't stop. She had kept singing, but not for him. This was why she came to church. To sing.

Suddenly she pushed him forward from behind so she could greet the Reverend herself.

"Thank you for the sermon," she said, avoiding his eyes. "It spoke to all of us, I'm sure. At least it should," shame now ridden with guilt for committing Noah's sin, fearful the Reverend somehow had found out. Here he was preaching specifically to her.

The Reverend smiled.

"All these years Mary, and you have yet to give me a bad review." Then he remembered to commend her good fortune. "You must be pleased Mac is the Trout King once again."

At first Mary looked shocked and then confused. What? Didn't she know? She didn't know. Why not?

Now that she did, she didn't care except to keep her ignorance from showing. Quickly she recovered with pretense.

"Yes. It's good for him to have it over." Turning to her sons, "Come along!" and she ushered them away, MacGregor made to follow after or get left behind.

"Will I see you Wednesday, Mary?" the Reverend called. Too late. Either she was out of hearing or she chose not to hear. MacGregor had been right. Something was wrong with Mary. She was not herself.

CHAPTER FOURTEEN

THE FIGHT IN THE DARK

It was close to midnight and the two fishermen had been sitting outside for several hours adjusting their eyes to the dark. Already they were able to see far more than they expected.

"You sure you won't take your rod?" asked Front.

"No," Sam replied. "This is your expedition. I'll wear my vest, that's all. Was going to bring the net until I realized it wouldn't even fit around this monster's tail. No, you're the fisherman tonight so you carry the pole."

Front was reflective.

"Is this a foolish thing to do?" he asked.

"Perhaps."

"Maybe we shouldn't be doing it."

"Maybe not," Sam gently agreed.

"Probably won't get the fish to strike anyhow."

"Probably not."

"Even if we did get him on, he'd likely break us off."

"Probably so."

"Do you want me to do this?" Front hoped his father would help decide.

"I want you to do what you want to do."

"Does it all have to be up to me?"

"Yes."

"If I decided not to go would you be disappointed in me?"

"No." Sam would not be entangled that way either.

"You won't make up my mind for me, will you?"

"I can't do that. It's your mind, not mine. So it must be your decision."

"And also because this time it's different?" Front wanted his father to acknowledge the whole truth.

"That too. This time it's different."

"But you are coming with me?"

"Yes. The adventure of a lifetime is no time to be alone."

"And you'll be there to help me?"

"Yes. I don't know exactly how," Sam promised, "but I will be there for you."

Front took time to consider not going. It was late. It was dark. It was chancy. It was scary. That was it. He felt afraid. Of what?

"I'm scared of what may happened," he confessed.

"So am I."

"What are you afraid of?" Fear was not how he thought about his father.

"I don't know."

"That's what I'm afraid of too." The boy felt reassured now that he was not alone in fear. "Let's go!"

Sam stood up.

"You lead the way."

And Front did, his father walking close behind. It was slow going. What light the sky had given was blocked by foliage above. They groped along the forest path, feet probing for roots and stones, Sam occasionally stumbling, quietly swearing to himself, as blind to branches that brushed against his face from out of nowhere as to the hidden drops and rises that tripped him up.

"Damn! Could have sworn I knew this trail as well as the back of my hand," exclaimed Sam in a whisper, as though guarding the secrecy of their mission. "Might as well be walking backwards for all that I can see. I don't know how you keep your footing. Must be a gift of being young."

No. Front's greater sureness did not depend on youth.

"Practice," he explained. "Yesterday I walked this path three times with my eyes shut to get ready for tonight. Once we get to the river it will be easier. Less shade from the trees, more light off the water. We'll keep along the shallow side up to the pool. Walking in water won't be so hard as walking through the woods. We never look where we wade in the day, anyhow."

Sam was glad to have his son so confident. And right. Wading was essentially a blind skill, relying more on feel than sight, trusting feet to find a stable footing.

"I'm sure grateful you did your homework for this trip," he said. "Gives me a fighting chance of getting where we're going without lasting injury."

Front accepted the compliment without a word. He had done his homework. Not only rehearsed his way through the forest, but plotted a course up river that led them out just below the pool, around and onto a section of rocky beach relatively unobstructed by trees behind. A place from which he could safely cast far enough back to shoot forward line required to reach the rock face. This distance he had calculated too by knotting the line so his fingers could detect how far was far enough.

All of these preparations he described to his father in a hushed voice as they got situated, the man instructed to sit on a large rock about ten yards below where the boy had chosen to take his stand.

"All ready?" whispered Front.

"I'm ready if you are," Sam whispered back. "Good luck!"

A moment of silence passed like a prayer between them. At last, the man heard the cast begin whipping through the night air, back and forth, back and forth, then the abrasive hum of line speeding through the guides. "Click!" From somewhere in the blackness across the river came the sound of Desperation Special bouncing off the rock face, silently dropping into the water.

Now Front recalled the advice he had been given.

"Pull it like a popping bug, make a commotion. That's what the Cowboy said to do."

In short, sharp jerks the boy began to retrieve the fly across the dark, smooth surface, silver water splashing with each pull, catching moonlight so the lure was easy to follow.

No luck. Nothing. No response. Front was not surprised. After all, it had been a foolish idea. An inexperienced boy up against the most experienced of fish. Lifting his rod to pull the end of his cast from the water and cast again, his line hung up.

"Darn! I've got myself snagged," he muttered, tugging to free the hook.

"What did you say?" asked Sam.

"Nothing," Front replied.

Then the world changed.

Had he not let go the line while answering his father he would have lost the great trout then and there. As it was the fish stole all it wanted before the boy could act to stop the theft.

'Oh my God!' Front was appalled. 'What have I done? What do I do now?' The possibility for which he had prepared, in which he had never truly believed, was now upon him.

Sam saw the boy's body stiffen and heard the reel free spinning. This could only mean one thing.

"Hey! You onto something?"

No answer.

"You must be on to something!" Sam stood up.

Still no answer. Then came the despairing moan of his son's dying cry.

"I can't move!"

"What!" barked Sam. "What do you mean you can't move? Is it him? Is it the One?"

"I – I think so," stuttered Front.

"Then what the hell do you mean you can't move?" Sam did not want to hear what Front was saying. "This is no time for that, for God's sake. Not that! Not now!"

The line kept running out.

"I can't move my hands!" The voice was sobbing now. "They won't do what I tell them!"

"Okay! Okay! Don't panic!" reassured the man, all but overcome by panic himself, rising to the challenge of fathering his son. "It's Okay. Like I told you, Buck Fever can happen to anyone. Now listen to me. Your hands don't have to do what you tell them. You got that? Just tell me what's happening and I'll tell your hands what to do. Okay?"

"You'll tell me what to do?" Front clutched at the hope being offered.

"That's right," Sam repeated. "Tell me and then do as I say. We're a team now. We're in this together. Two of us against the One. We've got him outnumbered. Remember that. Now, do you still have him on?"

The reel had stopped unwinding. All was quiet except for night sounds singing from the woods around them and excitement pulsing in their ears.

"I'm not sure. It happened so fast. So much line has been taken."

Sam took charge.

"Let's see. You may have hooked him harder than you know. Lift your rod up and slowly reel it until you feel it coming to a stop. Then you stop."

Deprived of will power, Front felt like an automaton, able to follow instructions from his father, absolutely lacking any initiative to issue or execute orders on his own behalf. Mechanically he wound in line, each turn of the reel bringing him closer to what he dreaded and desired. The ambivalence was agonizing. He feared he would reel in a free line and he feared he would not. Hope contended against hope. To lose the One Fish was to lose the chance of a lifetime, while to catch anything so great felt overwhelming.

Like a winch, turn by turn, he drew the line in until it held and would come no more, fixed to some object deep in the headwaters of the pool.

"I think he's got me hung up. If I pull any harder I might break the leader."

"No!" yelled Sam. "Whatever you do, don't horse him! You don't catch a fish this size, if you catch him at all, by pulling. You catch him by holding on. That's your job, to keep holding on. Do you feel any movement at all? Any shaking or tugging back?"

Front felt the quality of tension on the line.

"It's like I'm hooked onto a big log with some very slight give to it."

Sam felt relieved.

"That's him all right. I'm sure that's him. Just hold steady. Don't yank. A fish like this is a test of patience, not of strength."

"I couldn't move if I wanted to," murmured Front.

"Right. I forgot." Sam remembered the condition afflicting his son. "Wouldn't that be something if Buck Fever turned out to be a blessing in disguise. Well, we'll see. Let's give him a few more minutes to wonder what to do at his end while we wonder what to do at ours. Got to find some way to get him up and running so we can tire him out. But what to do? What to do? Maybe – how well can you see?"

Front stared into the darkness.

"Not into the river at all. Along the bank some."

"Okay." The plan felt rudimentary, but it was the best Sam could contrive at the moment. "Here's what we'll do. Try and frighten him with noise. Walk slowly up to the head of the pool scuffing rocks as you go, recovering what line you can. The sound of those rocks shifting underfoot and getting closer may scare him into action."

Front did as he was bid, his father following no longer lowering his voice to preserve silence, keeping up a constant patter to hold the boy's attention with instruction, checking periodically to make sure he still had his son on: "Understand?"

Front nodded to signify he did, unable to communicate his understanding of something else. Something more difficult. He was as much hooked by the great trout as the great trout was hooked by him. Who had caught whom? He felt hunted as much as hunter. The line between them made it so. Shuffling along the bank he felt as though he himself was being reeled in, not the reverse. As though the great fish was drawing him toward an outcome he did not want but could not resist, toward a hurt of his own making that he could neither imagine nor prevent.

The sound of rushing water now increased as he approached where the river ran full tilt into the rock wall and where, from his own explorations swimming, he knew the bottom dropped off like a cliff . Into these depths his line disappeared, anchored to a living thing laying on the bottom, deliberating its next move.

If power of will had been restored to Front at this moment he would have wrenched the line free to free himself from the anxiety he felt, a wish he could not share because the contest had changed. Now it was between the great fish and his father, himself reduced to an instrument of the man in the battle of his dreams about which Sam had often spoken. The boy prayed for his powerlessness to continue. If will was as suddenly restored as it had been taken away, he might take this gift from his father, wounding the man with a disappointment from which he would never recover. The weight of this responsibility was as heavy on Front as the weight of the great fish.

"Now what?" called Front in a hollow voice.

Sam had no ready reply.

"Wait a while longer. We'll figure out something." Although the man did not know what. Desperately he searched his experience for some strategy to goad the fish into action. The sound of footsteps had disturbed it not at all. 'My God!' Sam thought. 'There will never be another chance like this.'

Minutes passed. Nothing happened.

Now Sam gave voice to his concerns.

"We can't afford to wait much longer cause time is on his side. Once light starts coming up it will be 'Nellie bar the door!' He'll see enough to bolt for home. Once across the way he'll break us off as pretty as you please. Only darkness keeps him where he is, and you and I can't hold back the dawn. No, there must be a way to provoke this fish to fight. An irritator, that's what we need. A fish irritator. What?" He swore at his own stupidity. "Take me for a fool! I've got a fish irritator! Never thought of it because I've never used it."

Frantically he searched several vest pockets before finding the notebook ring Ojay had given him earlier that summer. In his fingers, in the moonlight, it shone like precious metal.

"Now if memory serves," Sam's voice excited by the possibility of using her invention, "we just snap this round the line and let gravity do the rest. When it bumps the fish's nose the fish takes off. That's what Ojay promised. Course we don't know what to guard against. Panic an enemy and you give him an edge. So we'll be driving this one to extremes. Wish I could think of another motivation, but I can't. You willing to give this a try?"

"I'm willing," answered Front obediently, his will at Sam's command.

"Okay, now listen closely." Sam would tell him all he could. "First run this fish had was on the house. No charge. He caught you by surprise so you gave him no resistance. Remember how fast he took the line? Well this time he'll take it even faster, too fast for your fingers to control. You're going to have to regulate the tension by shoving the reel, handle first, against your side, making a drag with the pressure you create, keeping that pressure on 'til he stops flying. Then you wind in what you can before he takes off again. Got that?"

"Yes." The neutral tone of the boy's voice communicated numbness he still felt.

"If this doesn't stir him up we'll have to start throwing rocks. The last resort is always crudest." The man stepped up to where his son was standing, attached the ring to the line, watched it fall and enter the water, then stepped back to observe the outcome of this experiment.

Front could feel the ring vibrating the line in its slow, meandering descent, like a bomb lazily floating down upon a target about to explode.

"Any response?" asked Sam.

Front shook his head. Waiting was unbearable. The helplessness of waiting added to the helplessness already felt. The line stopped shaking. The boy tensed in expectation. All was still.

"Anything yet?" Sam was impatient.

"Nothing."

Sam couldn't understand it.

"You'd think knocking on his nose would bother him just a little!"

Suddenly the rod bent violently forward, down and up, down and up, startling the boy who now felt the strength of the great fish for the first time, shaking its massive head from side to side in protest over this foreign object rubbing against it.

Noticing at once, Sam muttered to himself.

"Now we're in for it," then shouted "let him run!" which the fish did, tearing off downstream as Front clasped the reel against his side to slow the spinning.

"That's it, keep the tension on!" encouraged Sam, knowing so slight a pressure would not soon exhaust such a fish. "If he breaks down river it will all be over, but I don't believe he will. Lived here too long to leave his wallow. You watch, he'll dog at the bottom of the pool then dash back up. No choice but to follow him as best we can for as many turns as he has strength to make. Keep the closest line you can and pray that darkness keeps him on our side of the river."

Exactly as Sam predicted was how the fight proceeded. For what seemed like a long hour the great trout tore from one end of the pool to the other stopping only a few moments between runs to try and rid itself of the ring, wildly thrashing becoming wilder still, tearing off again. Each time on the other end of the line, boy and man stumbled along the bank as fast as they could travel, up and down, lap after weary lap, recovering line only to have it taken out by another burst for freedom, the man providing an unbroken patter of encouragement and instruction to the boy who depended on his father's words for motivation and direction.

"I don't know if we're tiring him, but he sure is winding me," gasped Sam. "You holding up all right?"

"I'm Okay." Front's heart was pounding but he didn't notice, senseless to his state of being.

"I think he's beginning to slow." Sam wasn't sure if this was hope or observation. "We should be getting a glimpse of him before too long." And before long they did.

The last run was up into the rapids, into the deep cross currents created where the river hit the water recoiling off the rock. This time there was no protest against the ring. Boring down to the bottom the fish was sulking, holding fast.

"What now?" asked Front, afraid to find out.

Sam felt stymied.

"I don't know. Fish this big will fight their heart out only stopping when they're killed or close to it. What you pull in can be more dead than alive. The way he's dove into that whirlpool his next act will likely be his last. Browns don't usually jump," he continued, "so they – Holy Mother of God!"

Up out of the river, darker than the darkness around it, burst a huge shape like some prehistoric thing, rising full length upon its tail for man and boy to behold, rising into the air, wavering, toppling, crashing back smashing the water, exploding sound and spray all the way down to where the two fishermen stared mute with wonder, each differently altered by what they had seen.

The line became slack. Automatically, without noticing that he was acting unbidden by his father, Front reeled it taut and then, bending his rod back against the great weight, pulled as hard as he dared. Strain upon the leader approached the breaking point, then miraculously the weight yielded slightly and he quickly wound in what little he had gained. Pulling back again he reeled in a little more, repeating the process over and over, towing the great trout slowly to shore.

"He's coming in!" exclaimed Front to his father. "I'm bringing him in!" he shouted triumphantly. "What should I do?"

Sounding weak, Sam made a soft reply.

"It's up to you. You're the Trout King now. I'm done. I can't do any more. I can't go any further."

Glancing over Front saw his father collapsed more than sitting upon the rock he had originally taken when the fatal cast was made. Something about the man looked broken.

"Are you Okay?" asked Front. Something about himself felt mended.

"I'm – I'm all right." Sam sounded very tired. "Don't worry about me. You take it from here."

Turning back to finish the fight, Front felt strength of will surging back through all parts of his body thrilling him with pride at what he was about to accomplish.

The back of the fish broke the surface like the hump of some huge sea creature about to run aground, its mouth gaping open, absolutely enormous compared to the Desperation Special which the boy could now see deeply embedded in the trout's upper jaw. Suspended from the fly was the ring, the final contrivance without which so great a fish would never have been taken.

As victory approached Front missed his father's words urging him on, missed the man not being with him to share this final glory. Glancing over again Front beheld a figure bent over in defeat, head down, arms limply resting on his knees, played out, as spent as the great trout, only waiting for the fight to mercifully be ended. Front was all alone.

Something felt wrong. Looking back now at the great fish barely alive in the shallows at his feet, the creature's eyes caught his own and the gaze held. And held. The trout lay there. The man sat there. The boy stood there. None of them moved.

What next occurred was something conversation afterwards never made clear. The son was as certain it had happened as the father was certain it had not.

Staring into the eyes of the great trout, Front heard a cry -- at first from far off, then growing louder, coming closer all around him, a shrill wail of terrible pain arising from everywhere at once. It seemed to come from the woods, the dark sky, the river, the fish, his father, even from within himself, like an outpouring of lamentation over some grievous loss, like the cry of a living thing about to give up life.

Whose cry? Whose death? He could not tell. Only that he must act to save whoever's life it was.

"NO!" shouted Front, the sudden yell startling his father to standing as the boy reared back and with a 'crack!' broke the leader at the knot, the fly remaining fixed to where it was, but the ring falling off into the water as the great trout keeled over on its side.

"What?" exclaimed Sam in shock. "What did you do that for? You broke him off!"

Front was shaking all over as though he had just stepped back from the edge of an unforeseen peril.

"Didn't you hear that scream?"

"Scream?" asked Sam. "You mean your scream? Of course I did!"

"No," Front objected. "The one before. Didn't you hear that?"
Sam couldn't understand.

"I heard nothing. What are you talking about?"

"You must have!"

"I swear," vowed Sam. "I heard nothing."

The two stared at each other in mutual disbelief. At last Sam spoke.

"Well, whatever happened, you can still have your fish if you want him. He's not going anywhere under his own steam. Pretty much done in, I'd say. Take him to town and you can retire the title. Even MacGregor would concede you that."

Front saw the truth of his father's words. There lay the great trout expiring, stretched out upon the water, floating more on it than in it, the exposed gill feebly gulping in the one substance – air – that would hasten its demise.

Heaving down his rod, throwing it away, Front waded into the shallows pushing the heavy body out into deeper water with his legs. Leaning over, he hugged the great fish with his arms in a life saving embrace, turning it upright, straddling and forcing the trout underwater with his weight until it was totally submerged. Standing waist deep in the river, bent forward, hands pressed down on the creature's head, Front watched its gills slowly resuscitate the exhausted giant until the tail began to slightly wave as vitality returned.

From the shore Sam did nothing to help or interfere. It made no sense and yet it made all the sense in the world, catching the One Fish only to let it go.

Finally the boy straightened up.

"He's all right! He's going to be all right!"

Sam nodded. He could not speak. A confusion of emotions was causing him to smile and cry at the same time.

Up went the boy's arms high over head, fist clenched in celebration.

"Here he goes! There he goes!" as the great trout swam away into deep water and disappeared as though it had never existed at all.

"Praise be!" sighed Sam to himself, grateful for the gift of loss.

For a long time the two fishermen stood looking across the pool at the rock face now dimly visible in the darkness paling into dawn. Night was passing and with it their experience that already had the feel of a preposterous dream.

Turning about, the boy faced his father who lifted his hat in a deferential and sincere salute. Front nodded, acknowledging this tribute as honorably and justly given, then waded to shore, emerging from the river as from a rite of passage, where he met Sam, arms outstretched. Without speaking, the two men held each other for as long as it took their pent up feelings to silently express, the happiness, sadness, exhilaration, exhaustion but above all relief that the adventure they shared had been well concluded. Companions in a common quest they had seen it through, had each relied upon the other when each could not rely upon himself. And here they were, together at the end as they had been at the beginning.

"Well," said Sam, "we've been there and back, I guarantee! Don't imagine if we live another hundred years, which isn't very likely, we'll ever have another fishing trip like this one, you and I."

They sat down on the rocks, grateful the earth was there to support them.

"Looking at this pool," continued Sam, "it's hard to believe that behemoth lives in here."

"I believe," said Front, although he was not sure he did.

"Yes," agreed Sam. "So do I. Not so easy to convince others, I expect. Like your mother, for instance. What are you going to tell her?"

"How I heard a trout scream."

"Ah yes," Sam remembered. "Now that she would believe."

"Do you?"

"After tonight I believe you believe your senses. I just didn't hear what you did is all." This was as close to validation as Sam could come.

"I want to thank you," said Front. "Without you telling me what to do I couldn't have done anything. The fish was too much for me to catch alone. Your words got me through. Knowing you were there for me knowing what to do. That kept me going. If he hadn't jumped at the end I never would have gotten back into myself. Seeing him showed me he was real. 'Til then, I didn't believe he was an ordinary fish."

Sam shook his head.

"He wasn't. Until I saw him I thought he was and played him that way. His jump took the heart right out of me. When he fell back into the water part of me went with him. In a way you saved my life. I mean it. Don't know if my love of fishing could have survived the death of that animal."

"I didn't do it for you," Front felt bound to be honest. "Let him go."

"I know," Sam replied. "But you did it for me anyway. How does it feel to be the Trout King?"

Front shrugged off the title.

"Not so good. Catching so great a trout as we did, that was wrong. It was all trickery -- in the dark, with an Outrageous Fly, with Ojay's ring."

Sam nodded.

"No argument there. It was sneaky from start to finish. Of course it always is, the more so the bigger they get. But I know what you mean. Problem is, walking down to a river and calling a fish out to fight has never worked very well. Seems they don't have much natural inclination to socialize with us that way. Never have. If it weren't for fooling them, we'd never get together. Fishing truly is a tricky business."

This made Front sad.

"I wish it wasn't. I didn't before but I do now. Don't you ever get tired of playing tricks on fish?"

Sam smiled.

"Never. Because the contest, the real contest, is not between me and the fish. It never has been. The contest is between myself and my dumbfounding ignorance of trout. It's ignorance I'm up against, not fish. The real battle is for understanding."

Front had never heard his father talk about fishing like this before, and as he listened he realized how the sport did not mean the same to him. Fishing was about catching fish. That was all.

But for Sam there was more to it.

"Amazing, humbling really," he went on. "What all these years of study have added up to. Not much. I haven't actually learned a great deal more than I knew as a kid following a creek through a meadow in search of fingerlings. I tell you, there's a veil of mystery surrounding the behavior of these creatures that human beings will never penetrate no matter how we long we try."

"Has it been worth it?" asked Front, wondering the same question to himself.

"Oh yes, a thousand times yes. That's the challenge, don't you see, the secrets are so naturally hard to discover. All knowledge of any consequence is grudgingly given, including knowledge about trout. It's because we understand so bloody little that tricks become important. Like tonight. All we have is a combination of tricks that for some undetermined reason inspired that beast to react as he did. The plain truth is we don't know why. Theories? Of course we've got theories. Name me one human endeavor filled with more unproven theories than fishing. You can't. But you can't name one that is filled with more human inventiveness either. Tricks? You're darn right. Every fly I tie is one more trick to try, and I wouldn't have it any other way."

Front felt a vague exasperation.

"Which do you love more, creating tricks or catching trout?"

Sam laughed.

"Now that's a question Ojay is always asking me. Best answer I can give is if, on Judgment Day, this poor angler is allowed to stand before the throne of God charged with fishing his life away, my defense would be in my tackle box, not in my creel."

Sam lay back and closed his eyes to imagine this encounter.

"Lord, I'd say, if you've got just one moment let me show you a few of these curiosities I've put together over the small number of years you have so graciously allotted me. Now I know these don't amount to much. They didn't save any lives, advance any science, stop any wars. But being a creator yourself, maybe you can appreciate invention on a much smaller scale than your own."

"And the Lord would reply," smiled Front, unable to resist entering his father's fantasy, "Fisherman, justify yourself."

"You see Lord, you see this little brown and black one here," Sam held up his fingers as though holding out the specimen for observation. "The brown is squirrel tail, the black is off a skunk. A Mudgrub I call it. Supposed to imitate a worm I found a few seasons back laying on the bottom, washed off the bank during an especially wet August. For two solid weeks this darn fly took fish in mist and drizzle when nothing else would even get a rise. Never caught anything on it since, but that doesn't matter. Point is, like every other fly in this box, like every other fly I've ever tied, each one has been an honest attempt to make something that works in a business where nothing comes easy."

"And did these all work, these efforts of yours?" Front was enjoying his role as Inquisitor.

Sam also.

"No Lord. I won't deny it. They didn't. Some worked not at all. A few, like the Mudgrub here, were sensational for a short while. Most of them have been intermittent performers at best. Like people that way, if you'll forgive my saying so."

"All this life time spent fishing," Front turned the screws tighter. "It was all effort?"

"Well putting it that way Lord," Sam replied, "I'd have to admit fitting in a little relaxation here and there. A few idle moments of pleasure for its own sake. Now and then a dash of pure recreational fun. I only mean to say that over the long haul I have honed my craft, sharpening my skills, such as they are."

"And how are they?" Front wanted to know.

Sam paused to figure up an honest estimation.

"On a good day with the wind behind me I can keep up with all but the best of them. My flies may not be as elegant as some, but they shine with variety and do get the job done. Reading the river, I'm as literate as most. And I've learned a thing or two from losing good fish about catching them. What I want you to understand Lord, is that while the nature of this pastime may sound casual, the quality of my commitment is not. I have done all I could with the capacities you placed at my command. And I have done it with love."

"That sounds good enough for me," pronounced Front, acquitting his father.

"Enough or not enough," said Sam sitting up, "it's all this fisherman has to give. Now, light's coming up and hunger's coming on. What say you and I head home and cook us something to eat. My appetite's been resurrected and I'm ready for breakfast."

"So am I," agreed Front, slowly standing.

A patter of raindrops began to lightly pock the quiet surface of the water.   Sam glanced upward noticing heavy overcast settling above the valley, clouding the morning sky.

"Looks like we're in for a spell of August weather," he predicted. "Arriving earlier than usual this summer."

And so began over a month of steady rain.

CHAPTER FIFTEEN

A LOSS OF LOVE

As rain drove gently down day after day, night after night, the wood changed character to suit the weather's dampening mood. Each hour of daylight was dulled to almost dusk by the prevailing mist, the forest growing darker as penetrating moisture turned gray bark to sodden black. The sound became muffled as soaked earth softened underfoot, excess wetness it could not absorb gathering into shallow pools overflowing into rivulets running for lower ground, finding drainage down small ravines and gullies, at last spilling silt and stray debris over the banks, turning the water slightly brown as the river slowly rose.

"Bad weather makes good fishing, so they say," pronounced Sam cheerfully, searching the evening drizzle for signs of clearing and discovering none.

"Who says?" asked Front. "Who's 'They'?"

"Nobody knows," answered Sam. "That's how folk wisdom works. Fishing is full of it. Sayings passed down through word of mouth, simplified through repetition until they sound like truth."

"Is this one true?" Sometimes his father's easy way with words was hard to trust.

"I hope so," Sam replied. "Because I'm going to need every edge nature can provide to lick MacGregor. High water sure could help. Flush those big fish from hiding, destroy their natural cover, and move everything around. A good flood could redesign the river and put Mac and I back on an even footing. He'd have as much to learn as me, even though he is ahead."

"I thought you'd quit the contest," interrupted Estelle surprised to hear Sam hadn't. "Front was the Trout King, you said."

"So he is," agreed Sam emphatically. "The three of us know that. But nothing we can say will convince MacGregor. Fishermen know better than to take each other at their word. Exaggeration is their style of speech. He won't believe what he can't see and he won't count what isn't weighed. As far as Mac's concerned, he's still the Trout King until proven otherwise. And I intend to be the man to do it."

To Estelle this made no sense, competing after the competition had been won.

"Why?" she asked. "What's the point?"

Sam's expression changed from relaxed to serious to grim.

"Because I don't like losing. Not eight years in a row. At first, it didn't matter. Fun was fun. Not anymore. Losing is one thing, getting whipped is another. I'm sick of it. And angry over how he treated Front. No. Just once. Just one time I want to beat MacGregor. Get him back the way he's gotten me!"

This was too much for Estelle, reviving an old complaint. Her husband was forever talking lightly about what she considered serious while treating what was frivolous as though it mattered.

"Honestly Sam, you sound like some of the boys I teach in high school who have to fight each other to prove they're men. Aren't you too old for this? Grow up!"

It galled Sam how she refused to honor the love of challenge that defined his life, man against man. Feeling criticized he criticized her back.

"Men don't outgrow their need for competition, Stel. And they never will. Being a woman you'll never understand!"

As with most of their disagreements, this one ended unresolved, each time they differed fracturing the marriage further, exposing more divisions harder to ignore, harder to discuss. Depending on Front to keep them together, Sam turning to him now as Estelle turned away. Front glad to be their refuge from conflict, wishing he was not.

"Going back to the west branch tomorrow," said Sam. "Want to come along? Only after garden variety trout this time. Nothing bigger than you or me, I promise."

Front smiled.

"Sure." Sometimes he felt grateful for his father's humor, the escape from tension it allowed.

"We'll fuel up at Ojay's on the way." Then Sam paused. "I believe she'd take it kindly if you forgave her. Only if you feel like it, I mean. I don't think she was out to do us in. Just putting family first."

Front understood and had made peace with what occurred.

"I'm not mad anymore. Besides, she gave us the ring. Funny how things work out so unexpectedly. I'd like to thank her, but I don't want her to know."

Sam was glad Front harbored no ill feelings.

"Forgiveness would be thanks enough. She acts crusty, but inside she cares." He finished up another fly he had been tying. "Well, I'm turning in," he announced. "I'll wake you early." Then to his wife, "Good night, Stel."

"Good night Sam." At least the courtesies in their relationship were still observed. One sign of caring that remained.

"If you want to get in bed. I'll read to you," she offered Front.

"Sure." Front never could predict what story his mother would select. Tonight it was a favorite from Robin Hood – how boastful Robin lost at quarter staffs to Little John. Front listened until Robin got his comeuppance and was swept into the water, bested by a better blow. He smiled and closed his eyes and did not hear his mother stop before the end.

Estelle tucked him in and then turned out the light. She felt tired herself. Tired of the bickering with Sam whenever either tried to talk. What had happened to all the old attractions? Turned into irritants. Sweetness gone sour. What they first liked about each other both had grown to find offensive. She used to love his sense of fun until she couldn't get him to be serious. He had admired her for being principled but now complained she was intolerant. Who was right and who was wrong? Perhaps they both were. The more they argued the righter each became.

Sam was asleep when she climbed into bed and he was out of bed next morning before she was awake, waking Front for an early departure, packing rubber ponchos to keep off the rain.

On the road father and son relaxed into each other's company. So many fishing expeditions they had shared, and here they were off on another. What would today's adventure bring? Sam smiled at the irony of his response.

"It sure feels good to fish for something small again."

Front pretended disappointment.

"You mean I can't expect to catch anything larger than the other night? Gosh, then what's the point of going?"

Sam played along with his son's playfulness.

"You can expect anything you want, but just remember mortal men are meant to fish for mortal trout. Go after what's reserved for gods and punishment will follow. At least that's what the myths say."

"Seems to me," Front slyly replied, "you caught that trout as much as me."

"Guilty as charged," agreed Sam. "A mercy you let him go. You let me off the hook."

"I'd do the same again," said Front. "He was too much of a good thing."

"Amen to that," added Sam as they pulled off the road at Ojay's. There she was. Leaning over the counter staring out the window. The same old sign adorned the door. IF I'M FISHING I AIN'T OPEN. IF I'M OPEN I AIN'T FISHING.

The same greeting when they entered.

"Morning gents. What'll it be?"

Front broke the ice at once.

"I've got a problem, Ojay. This man here," indicating his father, "he won't stop inventing flies. What should I do?"

To have the boy start gaming with her meant they were still friends and she felt cheered.

"Well son, it's a sad situation. Your dad's contracted a bad case of imagination. It ain't terminal, but it ain't curable either. He can't help playing make believe with artificial lures, while the plain and simple use of natural bait leaves him confused. I've about decided worms is too complex for him to understand – he can't tell one end from the other."

And so the old teasing began, all three enjoying the joking interplay that Front began, that Front was learning from his father, the fun of bantering, and so they laughed after breakfast over coffee.

"It's a training run today," Sam explained. "I'm going to get myself tuned up at the west branch to give MacGregor my best shot back here."

"You can tell him so yourself," said Ojay as a car rattled up outside. In a moment MacGregor heaved in looking worse from drinking more and sleeping less. It had been several weeks since Mary left his bed and he had found it hard to sleep alone. While during waking hours, ill humor made her hard to be around so he had kept away, staying out late and leaving early. He had barely seen the boys at all. Ojay's had become his home away from home, a place where he was welcome, given food, no questions asked, so he did not like being questioned now.

"Well Mac," Sam began, intending humor but once again unintentionally inflicting hurt, "don't tell me Mary's still starving you for breakfast?"

"Mary's asleep," MacGregor grumbled. Although how she slept so soundly at the kitchen table was difficult to understand. "And I'm up early as I always am."

"You better be," Sam wanted to put MacGregor on notice. To push himself he liked to push the competition. "Or else I'll get the jump on you. With the river rising, who knows what fish it may produce."

But this possibility was already on MacGregor's list of worries. He had seen late summer rains engorge the river and he knew what the river did in flood – drive smaller fish downstream before the current, leaving the bigger ones behind to feed. He knew the opportunities of swollen water as well as Sam, and the dangers better. And what he feared the most was that his rival, bent on victory and blind to risk, would dare to wade where caution should forbid and be rewarded for his rashness with a winning catch. MacGregor had suffered loss enough this summer without losing the title – the one remaining good among too much gone bad. But he pretended to spurn Sam's suggestion.

"You're talking desperate Sam. And when a man starts talking desperate, he's getting close to giving up."

Sam was not fooled.

"Believe that and you can relax. But you don't and you won't. No Mac, you've already been beat and you don't even know it. Now I'm going to give it all I've got. Three weeks left. May the best man win!" And with that parting shot he and Front left MacGregor to ponder Sam's warning words.

"What did he mean – already beat – do you suppose?" MacGregor asked Ojay when they were alone.

She had been curious too.

"We're missing something Sam's found out would be my guess. He must have hung a fish he's going back to catch. I wonder where?"

"I'll find out," intoned MacGregor. "I'll keep watch on where he's fishing. I'll find out."

Ojay said nothing, but she wished the summer over and the contest with it. The Reverend was right. It had become a 'cursed vanity'.

But not to Sam who had scheduled the day to test what flies worked best in heavy turbulence. He had been serious when he told Ojay this was a 'training run'. He planned to come away with the selection he would use back home. For his experiment he picked a different section of the west branch than they had fished before, one far too deep for Front to safely wade and so he must instead cast from the shore.

"I'll still go down below, even though you're not so likely to fall in. Better safe than sorry." Sam was more cautious with his son than with himself. "Your beloved dry flies would do well in this water. They don't need to float. You can fish them drowned." And Sam climbed his way downstream.

Front watched his father go and opened up the case of flies that he himself had tied, the ones that he knew best. He picked a blue dun parachute, enjoying how his fingers automatically twisted the leader after threading the eye of the hook, admiring the cleverness of the knot that caused the slippery nylon to pull tight against itself as strain upon the loop increased. Absently he made his first cast directly across the current and to his mild surprise took a fish immediately upon the fly hitting the water.

Soaring up into the air shaking its head leapt a rainbow the image of the one he'd caught before, both in size and the tactics it employed. Front eagerly anticipated the same excitement. This was a moment to thrill the heart of any dedicated fisherman, except the thrill was gone. He felt curiously untouched. The jumps, the runs, the dogging were all predictable. Dispassionately he worked the rainbow in, giving line when he had to, gaining line when he could, allowing the trout to deplete its energy by fighting the flex of the rod.

At last he drew the trout into the quiet eddy by the bank, the fish weakly finning, docile, played out of strength. Of caring. Then it struck him: so was he. Just another fish. There was no sense of delight, of accomplishment, of pride. Only of loss. He didn't care. What should he do? Was it right to keep a fish it did not pleasure him to catch? Of course his father would be pleased for him. But should he substitute his father's gladness for his own? He sighed. Then he did what his feelings wanted. Leaning down he wetted his free hand, grasped the creature tightly enough to appreciate its weight, and tucking the rod under his arm, with his other hand gently detached the hook. For the second time in a strange summer he released a trout that any fisherman worthy of the title would treasure keeping.

For the remainder of the morning Front cast intermittently, taking long breaks sitting down gazing at his damp surroundings, watching the rain fall, enjoying being by the river, grateful the river still called to him whether he fished or not.

Meeting his father for lunch, Sam asked the usual question.

"Any action?"

To which the boy responded in an unusual way. He lied.

"No. Nothing. How about you?"

His father showed him two good rainbows, both smaller than the one he had let go.

Telling a lie felt bad enough. Even worse was having it believed. The boy felt guilty for betraying his father's trust. But the alternative, faking enthusiasm or telling the truth, felt inadmissible. Caught in a bind of his own making, lacking a good way out, Front chose dishonesty and paid the price. He distanced himself to avoid discovery, driving home in silence with his father who respectfully observed the need for silence in his son. Not talking at a time they usually discussed the day felt lonely instead of close.

During the following week, Front made a few attempts to fish the river, on each occasion hoping to recover what he had lost, each time coming to a sad acceptance that he could not, finally giving up. Not going out at all.

"Is something troubling you?" Sam asked one evening as they sat out together on the porch.

Front shook his head.

"No." The question hurt because so did the answer. "Yes."

"You want to talk about it?" Sam could feel the feelings welling up inside his son.

"No."

"All right." Sam had the patience of a fisherman. He waited.

Front struggled with himself before confiding what he feared to tell.

"I feel all wrong. I don't know why." And he began to quiver with emotion, then to cry.

Reaching over Sam put his arm around the weeping boy and felt a stirring deep within himself, like pain, a sense of something precious breaking beyond repair.

Through a blur of tears the boy looked at his father across the gulf between them now.

"It's over!" he sobbed. "It's gone! My love of fishing. I've tried, but my heart's not in it. I go out to fish and end up sitting on a rock watching the water. Or the sky. I don't even want to catch anything anymore. What's wrong with me?"

Sam cocked his head up at the stars.

"I've noticed. Thought maybe you were looking for something up there, something you couldn't find in the river any longer."

"Like what?" the boy asked.

His father seemed to understand.

"Only you would know for sure," Sam gently suggested. "However, I've suspected you were searching for a new dream, the great trout having swam away with your old one."

"Dream? Why would I want a dream?"

"You don't want a dream," Sam explained. "People don't get a dream because they want one. Dreams are given and for better or worse, you're a dreamer. I ought to know, being one myself. Longing for something about which you can passionately care. Once you've felt it, anything less is never quite enough. Fly fishing for trout has been my dream most of my life. For a while it's been yours. Now I think that time is over."

Front protested.

"But I don't want it to be over! I want to love fishing as much as I did. As much as you do so we can keep loving it together. Now I don't. And now we won't. Why can't things go back to how they were?"

Sam could sympathize because it was a question he had often asked himself about his marriage.

"Why can't we go back? Because time's like the river. It only flows one way. We can fight the current but we can't reverse it. Going with the flow is what we have to learn to do. Giving up as we go along. Loss the name we give to letting go. Moving on is what you're doing now. Feeling the loss. Me too. I'll miss my fishing companion."

Front hated hearing the truth, but loved his father for telling it.

"Can't we ever go fishing again?"

"Of course we can."

"But it won't be the same?" Front felt obliged to be as truthful as his father.

"No." Sam would not contradict the question for the sake of comfort. "Not the same."

"The memories," Front asked. "Must we leave them behind as well?"

"No, and double No!" declared his father defiantly. "Whatever happens, they can't take those away from us!" Spoken as though 'they' were everything estranging that lay ahead in their relationship as the boy grew to manhood and he into old age. "No, memories like those we'll have to treasure whenever we choose. Each time we dig them up they'll shine more brightly than before!"

"And," Front halted, beginning to accept their old comradeship was at an end, worried how to fill the space between them now. "And we'll still be friends?"

"Oh yes," Sam promised. "We'll always be friends."

"Even though I'm no longer a fisherman?"

At this his father laughed out loud.

"No longer a fisherman? If it were only that simple! No, my friend, you don't get off that easy. Fishing forever catches the man who loves it. Make no mistake, you've been caught. For good or ill, whether for trout or for something else, you'll always be a fisherman. My God, I thought by now you'd understand: there's much more to fishing than catching fish!"

Sam was so rarely impatient with him that Front took this outburst right to heart. What *had* he learned from fishing? To love the outdoors. To enjoy spending time alone. To be patient. To be persistent. To savor anticipation, endure frustration, welcome success, weather failure. Most of all to commit his all to what he cared about. Listing what fishing had meant made him feel better. At least he wasn't leaving empty handed. Now if he could just find something else to do.

Over the rainy days that followed Front wandered restlessly from room to room through the small house, roamed the dank woods, even hiked up river further than he'd ever fished to where the surging stream crashed down like thunder from its mountain source in one cascading waterfall after another. This was a good day. He liked exploring unknown places, clambering up and over the big moss covered rocks, slippery from spray.

Back at home, however, the old dissatisfaction would return, made sad by seeing his father go off fishing each morning, the man now sharing less about his day because he and Front no longer shared the same pursuit, at night Sam tying flies alone. At night, Front's mother began reading to him more.

Boredom was what it was, a new feeling for Front and one not to his liking. A kind of loneliness arising from not being able to connect with himself or the world in a good feeling way. It was then that he began noticing Estelle. What she did all day. Not much. Mostly just sat around and read. Stacks of books, which grading papers and keeping house and family kept her from reading during school, she saved for summer. Curious, he asked how she could spend so long doing so little. Her response was not very satisfactory.

"Books take me places I love to go."

What places? Front could not imagine how sitting still could take you anywhere. Not that he could not read and did when school required. But he was more inclined to physical activities than to sedentary ones. More like his father. Still, the restless days wore on. Nothing to do. He wondered how his mother remained so content. He watched her reading when she was not watching him. Boredom was opening him up. Why not? Why not try to spend a day like her? To see what it was like. How much duller could it be than doing nothing?

Meandering through the living room after breakfast he noticed on top of the pile of books his mother kept in a basket by her rocker, one picturing a boy his own age in sailing clothes on the cover. He picked it up. Apparently unnoticing, Estelle kept reading. Trolling for interest.

"What's this about?" asked Front, not really wanting to know.

"Oh that?" she replied, absently glancing over. "It's a sea story. About a boy's adventure in search of buried treasure. About pirates. About one pirate in particular, Long John Silver. A very wicked man whom the boy comes to admire, perhaps even to love, in spite of the horrors this man commits."

"Should I read it?" Front wanted to be told.

"If you like." Estelle was prepared to give permission only.

"I wonder if I'll enjoy it?" Looking at least for some encouragement.

"I think perhaps you will," smiled Estelle, willing to give him that much of a nudge.

Front walked over to the couch by the window. Laying down he took a last look out into the gloomy woods toward the river. He sighed and reluctantly lowered his eyes to the first page, diving into the opening sentence:

> "Squire Trelawney, Dr. Livesey, and the rest of these gentlemen having asked me to write down the whole particulars about Treasure Island, from the beginning to the end, keeping nothing back but the bearings of the island, and that only because there is still treasure not yet lifted, I take up my pen in the year of grace 17 - , and go back to the time when my father kept the 'Admiral Benbow' inn, and the brown old seaman, with the saber cut, first took up his lodging under our roof."

Front read the long day through, swept away by the words, not stirring until at last he washed up at the story's end:

> "The bar silver and the arms still lie, for all that I know, where Flint buried them: and certainly they shall lie there for me. Oxen and wain-ropes would not bring me back again to that accursed island; and the worst dreams that ever I have are when I hear surf booming about its coast or start upright in bed with the sharp voice of Captain Flint still ringing in my ears, 'Pieces of eight! Pieces of eight!'"

It took a while for Front to return to his surroundings. So far away had he been transported. With some surprise, he noticed morning had become late afternoon. Where had the day gone? Dishes clattered in the kitchen. Stiffly getting up he wandered in to ask his mother if there were other books as good to read. She didn't know. Too dim to identify but too strong to deny, a new yearning began growing inside of him.

In fact, there turned out to be many more good books to read, captivating accounts of all kinds that kept mysteriously appearing on top of the basket by his mother's chair. When he would finish one another would be waiting, each as compelling as the last. There was an old man in a small boat on a vast ocean who caught a truly great fish. A boy washed overboard on an ocean liner, picked up by a fishing boat where he learned to practice that dangerous trade. A dog that became wild and led a pack of wolves, and a wolf that became tame to the hand of man. Story after story catches his imagination, losing his sense of passing time.

Thus Front was surprised when Sam announced they would be leaving in another week. The boy took the news better than his father.

"Not much time left!" Sam complained.

"For what?" asked Front. He had forgotten about fishing, the contest, and his father's challenge.

A good sign, thought Sam.

Not so the weather. The rain instead of letting up was pouring down.

CHAPTER SIXTEEN

VERDICT BY THE RIVER

With the torrential rain, the river filled its banks and spread and flattened out into a smooth expanse of muddy water winding serpentine along the valley floor, a broad brown snake deceptive in its subtly and power that warned most fishermen away, but tempted one.

Sam Henry knew the river's character in all its temperamental moods, so he believed and so informed his son and wife, forbidding it to Front because of danger, while assuring Estelle that he himself was well experienced to fish with caution, forgetting how carelessness was born of confidence.

"Are you sure it's safe with the water up so high?" she asked. In summers past he had quit the river when it rose to flood.

"Don't worry, Stel. It's as safe as a fisherman is mindful. I won't take any stupid chances."

But Estelle was skeptical.

"Yesterday Mr. Detmer told me taking any chance was stupid when the river was so treacherous. He was disturbed you'd even think of trying. He said no fish is worth the risk you would be taking."

"With all due respect to Mr. D.," Sam demurred, "he's just wanting the title for the town. Like the rest, all in cahoots, the whole town against me. I've learned that much this summer. Now even Nature's siding with MacGregor. But I'll beat the lot of them!"

For Sam to be so stubbornly combative infuriated her. In Times like this there was no getting through.

"You just won't listen, will you? Not when you don't want to believe. Mr. Detmer was truly concerned!"

"I'm sure he was," agreed Sam sarcastically. "But not for me." Discussion ended.

Estelle may have had wrongs on her side of the marriage, but she was right in this: once Sam made up his mind there was no changing it, even when ignoring peril could lead to harm. Like with the river.

Like with MacGregor. Too many years spent looking on the bright side had blinded Sam from recognizing the presence of the dark. The self-fulfilling prophecy he followed so successfully at work – expect the best and the best will follow – caused him to minimize and disregard the worst. The result was a badly misunderstood relationship.

He could no more imagine MacGregor capable of malice than MacGregor could believe Sam was not prepared to do him in. Why not? MacGregor was not daft. The evidence spoke for itself. There were the hints that Sam had dropped. There was the challenge he had given. And most of all, there was Ojay's opinion: Sam must have found a bigger fish that he was going back to catch.

Damn the man! Why couldn't Sam let well enough alone? MacGregor felt bone-weary, a champion beset by unrelenting competition. He knew his notoriety lasted no longer than his winning, and that he could not win forever. But he could ill afford the costs of a defeat. To Sam Henry, the title mattered little, while to MacGregor it was most of the respect he'd earned.

So he drank and spied. Early morning, lunch, and late afternoon, taking breaks from work, he would patrol the river until he scouted out where Sam was fishing, noted the location, and observed the man remaining unobserved himself. Once he saw Sam, wading on the edge of safety, snag something promising that thrashed the surface, dove and ran with the ferocious current, breaking free because no fisherman could fight this river. Pleasing and worrisome as well. Conditions were impossible, but there were big fish hunting in the maelstrom to be caught.

Thus far MacGregor found no pattern to where Sam put in, no one spot he returned to more than any other. Of course there were no traditional locations to be seen. The river had become unrecognizable from the stream it used to be. The Railroad Shallows were shoulder deep and rising. At Grisham's Well, the dogleg had been straightened out. Call it Grisham's Run. While at the Riverbend, the rushing water had attacked more than half way up the granite wall and angry that its siege had failed, had turned with vengeance to pillage the opposing shore.

In the evening Mary would notice how MacGregor staggered home soaked to the skin and wondered why, but would not ask lest expressing interest sound inviting. Nor did he share the worry deviling his mind that drove him daily to spy upon his rival in the driving rain. He knew it was a crazy thing to do, but also he'd feel crazier if he did not. What good could watching do? No good he hoped. He was after doing bad. So he put faith in superstition, maybe his malevolence could spoil Sam's luck. Only a few days left to go. After that Sam was free to catch the most enormous trout God could create for all MacGregor cared. Out of season was off the record. Out of season and he was safe.

Preoccupation with the contest also kept MacGregor from keeping the boys at work. He let up assigning jobs or when he did, forgot to check if they had been accomplished. As for Mary, she too disengaged. Because she stayed up late she woke up later, wishing she could hide her eyes from the disorder worsening about her, her home her image of herself.

Bravely she would attempt to put away and throw away but there was no 'away' that she could find. She had only rearranged the mess.   Soon, discouraged by the futility of trying, she felt overwhelmed, then helpless, then depressed. What was the use? Reaching for the answer, she slumped down and began sipping slowly to stop feeling worse, slipping gradually into a daze, briefly revitalizing when MacGregor dared appear, relapsing back when he was gone. He didn't stay for long.

Both boys saw the changes, but what troubled Goeff was irrelevant to Gordie. A new freedom ruled the house as rules were given up. Now there was freedom from neglect. Already detached from his surroundings, Gordie neither liked nor minded this alteration in his world because whatever happened was all the same to him. He could not be touched. Not any more.

For Goeff, however, this freedom was a prison of responsibility. Who else was left to do housework except himself? And if he didn't, what would become of home? So he relied for help on Gordie who willingly followed so long as he was led, offering no objection, but doing nothing unless told. The responsibility was Goeff's alone. Alone and lonely. Each member of the family isolated from each other as binding ties began to strain and fray and break.

To hell with family! This was how MacGregor felt. A lot they cared, so why should he? He had his work to do and Sam to watch, and fraternizing when the day was done. Only a few more days and then this torment would be over. My God, he'd never seen such rain. It didn't pour, it waterfalled from clouds too full to keep the deluge back. Not even Sam could fish in a monsoon like this. Roads were awash like drainage ditches, while the river had begun to surge in waves. No. Surely Sam knew better than to tempt the elements with nature running riot. All the same, just to make sure, MacGregor would go check and see.

But the going was slow and the seeing not easy. Fording a flooded crossing was how driving felt – creeping in lower gear hoping wetness would not stall the motor out. There was so little visibility he could not see the river from the road, only the roadside dimly, but that was good enough. He would look for where Sam parked his car.

Damn! There it was. Maybe he was in it. MacGregor drew alongside. No! The Devil take him! Here's to the Devil! MacGregor took a long pull off the bottle to fortify himself against the weather, strengthening his will at the expense of judgment.   Then, loudly cursing, he climbed out into the drenching rain, into the roaring sound of rushing water growing louder as he slogged toward the bank, one hand across his forehead, a visor for his eyes, searching for his enemy, wishing him ill.

There he was! MacGregor could not believe it. Stranded in the middle of the raging river, Sam was casting as if weather had been balmy and the water clear and low.

Actually MacGregor was deceived. Sam was not fishing so carelessly as he appeared. In truth he was a prisoner of where he stood and knew it, victim of his own miscalculation. Sam had made a false assumption in a situation intolerant of error. Logic had promised the path that he had followed in would be there when he wanted to return, but logic was mistaken as he discovered wading back to shore. The path was gone. There was deeper water all around. Whatever route his feet found in they lost to lead him out. And it was on their feel and understanding he must depend since the bottom was concealed beneath a murky cover.

Trapped. Remain where he was and water girdling his chest and lapping higher would suck him down. Retreat from whence he came, as trying had disclosed, only threatened to deepen his dilemma. What should he do? Not a man easily given to dismay or panic Sam surveyed as much of his immediate surroundings as heavy rain permitted until a patch of creamy colored water caught his eye, not far beyond, not far below where he was so precariously placed. The lighter brown signaled a shallower stand if he could reach it without mishap which he barely did, losing contact with the bottom briefly before recovering his footing on a bar of sand, rescued for the moment in water fallen to his waist.

Concern for his predicament did not trouble Sam for long. Strong denial of the negative forbade considering dire implications of his plight. Positive thinking was the answer. Everything would be all right. Look on the bright side. What you believe is what you get. What could be better? Here he was perfectly positioned to cast to either bank, up stream or down. What more could he want? Only one thing, a fish to take the title from MacGregor.

But making light of danger does not make danger go away. In truth he was marooned on an island of sand eroding underfoot, sinking him down while the foment grew wilder about him.

"Sam!" yelled MacGregor. "Get your ass to shore before you drown!" But the words were silenced by the uproar of the river and the downpour of the rain. "Damn fool!" Was it sheer stupidity or blind ambition that drove Sam to such daring?

Glancing upstream for an instant, MacGregor instantly beheld the answer. The magnitude of what Sam was concealing became maddening clear. Lolling sideways down the tumult, rolling like a log, was no ordinary fish but a trout the size that myths are made of and records permanently set.

The great trout it was. Too old to recover from the fight with Front, it was too weak to withstand the flood that had flushed it from the Riverbend along with all the other debris. Having fought the river for the right to remain where it had long belonged and lost, the giant fish was hardly more than detritus itself, barely alive, set adrift, half submerged and horizontal in the current, one end bobbing up and moving forward then the other. No wonder Sam mistook it for a log.

Casting diagonally to avoid the floating object he snagged it nonetheless as a sudden blast of rain swept across the river blowing his line back where he had not intended. Jerking to free his fly, instead he hooked it deep.

Too much for MacGregor. The old poacher could detect a fish in any natural disguise and he knew a cunning cast when he had seen one. Then drunken fear decreed what must be done.

"No-o-o-o!" he bellowed and thrust himself into the torrent wading where he could and swimming where he must, closing in on his rival from the side as the great trout closed from above. Just when MacGregor's arms clinched Sam in a boxer's hug, the giant fish slammed broadside into both, upending them together as down they went and under, rolling over, first Sam above and then MacGregor, gasping for air but inhaling water, choking, gagging, swallowing what each meant to spit out as the river bore the two away in a tangle of senseless anger and stupid competition.

Shackled by an overpowering grip that could only be MacGregor's, Sam did not waste precious energy trying to free himself from what could not be broken, while his captor held on to Sam for dear life or death or whatever he intended. Theirs was a roller coaster ride with no getting off, sinking down and madly fighting for the surface, up and down, with the worst hazards laying hidden underneath.

While the river presented a smoothly flowing cover, the contours of the riverbed and boulders on the bottom created a havoc of currents at war below. It was these tows and pulls that tugged and tore at the two men, that drew them down as they kicked and twisted desperately to reach a re-supply of air before the water smothered them again.

On one such downward plunge cruel mishap struck, a rock stunning the victim leaving the other man to save them both if he could bring them up in time to breathe. The effort took the last of his remaining strength, so when they broke the surface he was as spent as the other man was insensible. There was no struggle left in either one. The fight was over. The river won and they had lost. To sink once more would mean they would not rise again.

Except the river offered rescue after it arranged for death. While flood had straightened out much of its winding course, a few of the larger bends remained, and it was into one of these the men were mercifully swept, flung to the curve's perimeter that spread beyond the bank and shallowed out over what had been a dry grass meadow. There, along the edge, where muddy water made a muck of muddy ground, they were deposited with other flotsam from the flood, left as evidence to mark how far out of its banks the little stream had strayed.

Neither man moved. Both were still wrapped together, covered with sediment from the turbid water, coated brown by the mire in which they were embedded. Finally the two fell apart as one of them rolled over, lay still, slowly raised himself to see what happened, saw his mate unmoving, and scrambled over on all fours to get him up.

Shaking the sleeping man he called his name, lifted his head and shoulders, felt the dead weight, lowered it slowly to the ground, pleaded for God's sake one last time for him to wake. Damn the man! Why didn't he wake up? No use. No breath left in the body. Standing up he bent and dragged his companion several steps, halted, then dragged some more until he reached the highway. There he left the lifeless laying and trudged into town.

There were no cars for him to flag for help and if there were it was unlikely anyone would stop to aid a frightful looking swamp thing like himself, a man in the fantastic make-up of a monster staggering drunk with fatigue down the center of the road.

Certainly Mr. Detmer did not first recognize the figure for a man, and when he did could not discern what man it was. The old proprietor had been rocking on the porch, back and forth as regular as an old town clock, pondering the rain and thinking maybe it was letting up at last. Bad for business, this much rain. Kept folks inside content to do without rather than risk driving, getting out, and getting soaking wet.

What was this? Something tottering down the deserted street. A man. What man? He pushed himself out of the rocker and stepped forward to the edge of the porch. The strange figure bore the look of a survivor or the bearer of bad news or both. A dreadful sense of premonition gripped Mr. Detmer as he waited for the future to approach and reveal itself.

"He's dead!" the man drew close enough to speak, hoarsely repeating, "He's dead!"

Mr. Detmer didn't recognize the voice until beneath the mask of mud he recognized the face.

"Mr. Henry! Is it you? What happened? Wally, come out! Wally! It's Mr. Henry and there's something wrong! Give us a hand!"

When a man who never raised his voice is moved to shout, then others who have never hurried may be moved to run. Wally was out the door and on the porch quicker than his wife thought possible, she close behind, followed by her mother.

"Bring him inside!" ordered Cora.

"No. You don't understand!" protested Sam, gasping from the strain. "MacGregor's dead! He tried to save me from the river and he drowned!"

The news struck Mr. Detmer like a blow. His legs gave way and he collapsed to sitting on the steps. His prophecy of harm had been fulfilled and he felt a terrible responsibility. If he could prophesy why couldn't he prevent?

"Mary!" recalled Cora who was concerned about the living. "Who's to tell Mary?" Not wanting it to be herself.

Seeing his wife at a momentary loss, Wally proved his dependability once again. He carried on.

"I'll go fetch Ojay and the Reverend. We'll do nothing 'til we've talked with them. But I better wait to get Mrs. Henry, after we've gotten Mr. Henry some cleaned up."

This was a task Cora could gratefully accomplish. By the time Wally returned Sam had been scraped and sponged and fitted into an old pair of Wally's overalls and sneakers, a little large but clean and dry, improving his appearance back to human, although he was still in shock. Deprived of the easygoing speech that he traded on in public, he sat collapsed, mute with exhaustion.

The Reverend put his hand on Sam's slumped shoulder.

"I'm glad you came through. I'm sorry about MacGregor." Nothing more that he could say. His loss of friend hurt far too much for him to openly express.

Ojay had volunteered to drive with Wally to get Estelle and Front because she wanted to prepare the boy as best she could. He had remained her friend and she wished to honor what that friendship meant. MacGregor was another matter. The town would not be the same without MacGregor. Like most everybody else, she didn't feel she knew him as a person. More of an actor in the role of local character, a walking uproar of a man. Except these last two weeks when she had fed him regular. Then she discovered a loneliness about him to which she could relate. Now there was only Mary. That would be hard. What would become of Mary and the boys?

As Wally parked outside the Henry's summer bungalow she saw Front standing in the yard staring up in wonder at the sky. The rain had stopped.

"Ojay!" Front was glad to see her. "What are you doing here? My Dad's off fishing."

"I know," replied Ojay, opening the door. "Your father's had a bit of luck – some bad, some good. Bad is, he lost his footing in the river. Good is, he managed his way out."

"Is he Okay?" Front was alarmed. "Is he hurt?"

"Ain't hurt," Ojay promised. "Just wet and shaken up. He's waiting for you and your Mom at Detmer's. We come to get you."

"Mom!" shouted Front. "Come here!"

Estelle was out the door almost before her son had finished yelling.

"What's wrong?"

Quickly Ojay repeated what she had told the son. But Estelle wasn't fooled.

"There's something more. What aren't you telling us?

Ojay wished the wife was not so sensitive.

"MacGregor drowned trying to save your husband."

"My God!" Estelle grabbed Front as though she never meant to let him go. Her husband had survived when he could easily have died. The closeness of the call frightened her into clinging to her son. Together they climbed into the back seat.

Nothing was said on the drive to town. Each was contemplating what was necessary next. Front, while trusting Ojay's word, needed to see his father to make sure he was alive. Estelle also needed to see Sam, but as much for the marriage as for himself. Wally needed to keep plodding through unpleasant tasks that tragedy created. Someone must go and fetch MacGregor's body. Who but himself? While Ojay must do what she could for Mary. The family would need someone to stand in for MacGregor. And to admit the truth, Ojay stood in need of family.

It was Front who reached his father first, who held on and on and on. Estelle had to wait her turn. Child before parent. The order struck her as appropriate. Love from and for a child was so much more uncomplicated than between husband and wife.

Her turn at last. It was with difficulty Sam met her eyes.

"I did a stupid thing after all," he confessed. "An awful stupid thing. I got in too deep and pulled MacGregor with me. He fought the flood for both of us, but even he was no match for the river." And Sam began to cry.

Estelle was not used to seeing her husband broken open with emotion running out. Not the cheerful, glad-handed man that she had married. Not the man she thought she knew, so she did not immediately respond.

"Let's go home," she said at last. "Wally, would you drive us one more time?" Wally would. And tomorrow would take one of them to get their car.

As they filed out, Estelle hovering close to Front, Sam lagged behind shopping for something before he left. Something not on the shelf. He paused by the old cash register where Mrs. Detmer had resumed her perch.

"Well Mrs. D., what would the Bishop have to say?" the question asked in sadness, in bewilderment, not humor. The old woman knew the question would be coming because it was one she had asked herself.

"The Bishop was a mighty understanding man, Mr. Henry. He would be grateful you survived and he would mourn MacGregor's loss. And he wouldn't blame the living for the dead."

What Sam needed to hear.

"Thank you Mrs. D. I'll try to remember that." And he straggled out.

Watching Wally leave to take the Henrys home, Cora reflected as she occasionally did, on how gracefully he eased people along when difficulty struck. Nothing dramatic. Just providing little acts of service that enabled them to pass through trouble smoothly. Hardly noticeable help, and yet invaluable. A capacity to keep things moving when others might lose motivation or get stuck. Keeping things moving was Wally's gift. Steady working, unhurried, even tempered, infinitely patient, he was a man on whom she could daily depend to do as he was told and to think of doing what she had not foreseen to tell. Reliable and uncomplaining to a fault just like her father. Easy to take them both for granted. At times like this she meant to give her husband credit he deserved, but as always something else took priority. How would she break the news to Mary and shore the broken family up.

Ojay and the Reverend were awaiting what she had to say because they knew Cora could not give help without taking control of the arrangements.

"We'll go together," Cora announced. "Mary's not used to visitors so she'll know something's wrong. That can't be helped. If they can count on you for breakfasts, Ojay, I'll fix the suppers and bring groceries for lunch."

"At my place or theirs," answered Ojay. "It don't make no difference."

"Reverend," continued Cora, "the funeral service is up to you. Don't overdo it. I won't have Mary put through more than she can take. She's not been well and this will only make things worse."

"I'll be brief," the Reverend promised, promising himself a service through which he could express the loss of friendship that he felt.

It was how Cora had foreseen. One friend arriving unexpectedly was disturbing, but a delegation was alarming. Mary leaned against the door holding herself up, bracing for whatever tidings these messengers would bring.

"Now Mary," insisted Cora, "we'll all go inside and sit down. You two come along," this last to Goeff who looked suspicious and to Gordie who was watching shafts of sunlight shooting through the clouds.

Despite Goeff's efforts, the kitchen was a mess. Neatness of one was no match for the untidiness of three. While Cora seemed not to notice, nor the Reverend, Ojay saw in the disorder symptom of a world gone wrong.

"Mary, boys," began Cora not knowing how to speak except directly, "we have bad news. MacGregor's dead. He was trying to save Sam Henry from the river and he drowned."

In the stunned silence following this announcement Mary stared in disbelief at Cora, at the Reverend, then at Ojay who murmured softly.

"It's the truth Mary. I wish it wasn't."

Mary still could not comprehend. Now she glanced at the boys to see if they had heard what she thought she had heard. Goeff's hard face was darkening in anger, while Gordie smiled as tears wept softly down his cheeks.

It must be true. MacGregor was not coming back. Was gone. And strangers come to bear the news. Only they were friends. All three awaiting some reply, some sign. But she couldn't cry. She hadn't any crying left. How could she explain her feelings for MacGregor were already dead? That all her crying had been done. She felt dead herself. She couldn't.

"Thank you," Mary simply said. "Thank you for coming out." She pieced her thoughts together as she spoke. They were disorganized. "It's sudden news. We need some time. We'll have to make some changes. A lot to do."

Cora interrupted.

"Now Mary, don't worry about fixing meals. Ojay and I will take good care of that. As for the funeral, the Reverend here will look to the arrangements. What happens later we'll work out after the funeral is done. We'll find a way to manage, you may be sure."

"We will," echoed Ojay. "Would you like some time alone?"

Mary numbly nodded and the deputation got up to go, last to leave the Reverend, hanging back.

"Was something wrong between you and MacGregor at the end?" he gently asked. "You can tell me if you want. It might help ease the pain."

Mary shook her head.

"Nothing important, Reverend. Nothing that really mattered. Nothing that matters now. Only a quarrel. In time we would have made it up." Which is what Mary wanted to believe. They just ran out of time.

"Well, if you need to talk," the Reverend patted her on the arm. "The funeral day after tomorrow? Or is that too soon?"

"That would be fine," she agreed, to free herself of company. To free herself from other people's questions to confront her own. Had she done wrong? What if the misdeeds she held against MacGregor were not deserving of how she punished in return? What if they were not as bad as she remembered? They had only happened once. Had she relented, would they be together now? What if it was her unforgiving nature that, driving him from home, drove him to the river and to his death? Mostly he had been good to her. Why should a little bad count more than a lot of good? What if it was all her fault?

"He left us in a sorry fix, he did!"

The harshness of the tone tore Mary from her thoughts. It was Goeff speaking, spitting out the words.

"A lot he cared! Save Mr. Henry and the hell with us! Well to hell with him, I say! I'm glad the bastard's dead!"

Too much. In defense of caring she didn't know she had, Mary swung around in fury and Goeff felt his head whipped to the side, stung by the flat of his mother's angry hand upon his face.

"Never let me hear you curse your Da' again!" She was trembling with rage. "He died a hero. More than that, he was the Trout King. And don't you forget it!"

CHAPTER SEVENTEEN

THE END AND THE BEGINNING

The morning of the funeral broke dazzlingly clear, the air cool and crisp, shimmering with renewal after so many days of cleansing rain. The sky, the woods, and the sun, restored to their original resplendence, shone their truest colors – crystal blue, lush green, and blinding yellow. The earth was deeply satisfied and yearned to be replenished.

Flood? What flood? Only a winding line of litter now remained to mark how high the river rose, a line that wind and time would soon erase. Not so the memory of the man MacGregor. His loss was felt all over town. Already history had begun to do its lying work.

Unlike living in the city where so much dramatic happened that little was long remembered, in Bishop's Place significant events were few and far between. Prized for their infrequency, they were immediately entered into local lore to keep a sense of shared experience alive, landmark events to date time as it passed, this summer easy to remember -- the Great Rain, the Great Flood, and the Drowning of the Trout King. Local history was always revising the past to suit the present, creating triumph from adversity and heroes out of ordinary folk, producing a common heritage the town was proud to own.

Like the Bishop. Not a day went by when someone did not invoke his name, recall some outrageous act or kindly word attributed to him. Who knows which tales were true and which made up? Who cared? Accuracy was not the point. The qualities he stood for were what mattered, and what the telling of the stories meant. To make reference to the Bishop was to belong to Bishop's Place.

And now more history was in the making. The Legend of the Trout King was beginning to be told as MacGregor, the man to be remembered, began to replace the man whom gossips had actually known, his unpleasant side discarded and his accomplishments enhanced. MacGregor may not have been well liked in life, but in death he left a legacy to last for years to come. Now he wouldn't have to earn his reputation anymore. It was secure.

So the whole town turned out for MacGregor's funeral, filling the little church to overflowing, as by paying tribute to MacGregor they were paying tribute to the town and to themselves. To be present at his memorial was to witness history. All of which the Reverend knew. They were not here out of friendship for MacGregor. They were all acquaintances. He was the only friend. And his job was to celebrate the man as best he could so they could leave appreciating him, while Mary and her sons could come away supported by the town. Tricky to do because he glimpsed too much unhappiness at home to praise MacGregor within family. So he elected to commemorate loss of fisherman and friend instead.

Not the entire congregation was from the town. Some summer families for whom MacGregor worked were there, also the Henrys who received almost as much attention as Mary and the boys, but of a different kind. While looks and words of condolence were warmly given to the widow, cold disregard was leveled at the Henrys, particularly Sam who might as well have had an albatross hung round his neck. He killed the Trout King, was the condemnation that he felt. And his presence was unwelcome here.

Suddenly the congregation hushed. Down the aisle unsteady on her feet shuffled Mary, Cora on one side and Ojay on the other, leaning upon her friends like crutches, followed by a vacant looking Gordie and a glowering Goeff. Because of Mary they made a slow procession, one uncertain step and then another down to the front. Cora cast a stern eye at the Reverend to remind him of her charge. In compliance, he had omitted any music to spare Mary having to stand and sing. He would keep it simple. A few words was all.

Before he spoke he smiled reassuringly at Mary, then began.

"Today we gather to honor the memory of Alexander MacGregor who risked his life to save a life and died. For most men this would have been an act of courage, but bravery requires overcoming fear, and MacGregor did not know how to be afraid. It was a feeling foreign to his nature. He was a grappler. He wrestled with the challenges life gave him, no holds barred, trying whatever worked and if it didn't trying something else. You couldn't break a thing too bad he couldn't fix, and he made this boast the basis of his trade.

"Each of us in Bishop's Place has grown to know MacGregor. How could we not? We had no other choice because he gave us none. Not the sort of man one could ignore. His own person he was, and outspoken about it. He courted no man's favor and no man worked harder for his family's keep. From that first day he drove into town with Mary and two small sons, Bishop's Place was not the same. We all had to make room for this hulking new arrival, larger and brasher than most of us, larger and brasher than life.

"Myself, I met MacGregor on the river and we got along. Which doesn't mean that we saw eye to eye. We argued more than we agreed, arguing his way of making talk. But we liked to fish together, so we did.

"You know, when you fish beside a man for many years a bond develops that you never quite appreciate 'til it is lost. Then you say to yourself, 'well that's gone. And I'll never have the like again.' And life goes on and you go on without your friend. And I'll go on without MacGregor, but it will take some getting used to. Men have a way of making friendship over fishing that comes of growing comfortable with one another. I'll miss him by the river in the afternoons.

"Now this is not the kind of talk to use in church, what I'm about to swear, and I the minister, but this much must be said. MacGregor was one hell of a fisherman. Not because he strove to be. He didn't. But because fishing was born and bred into his nature. By instinct and by necessity.

"All the ways there were to capture fish, MacGregor knew and mastered every one. 'Poor Man's Meat' is what he called the trout, there to be taken when there was nothing else to eat. What lack of money could not buy, nature would provide for him who had the craft to catch it.

"I've seen him lure and bait and drive and trap and even catch fish with his hands, creeping up and under from behind. Trout King? We may have originated the contest, but MacGregor owned the title long before. Then he held it for the town against all comers, every year, through good luck and bad, in every kind of weather, drought and flood.

"And in honor of the honor that he brought us, may we stand by his family now. May we say to Mary, henceforth you are one of us and we shall help you carry on. And to Gordie and to Goeff, your father was a hard man to follow. but he beat a broad path and there are those among us to guide you on your way. Now let us pray."

The prayer was made in silence, "each in his own heart, each in her own way" because the Reverend did not want to profane the spirit of his friend with religious words, respecting MacGregor's antipathy to sentiments that sounded holy. Then he stepped down from the pulpit and walked over to face Mary who was bent forward, apparently unwell, securely held from falling by her friends.

"Nicely done Reverend," said Cora. "You kept your word. Now lead us out. We need to get her home to rest."

"Come Mary," urged Ojay in a whisper. "Soonest out is soonest over."

Mary let herself be pulled to standing and then, with an expression both dulled and determined, step by halting step, she faltered up the aisle until she stopped abruptly, threw off her supports and turned aside to face some member of the congregation.

"You!" she hissed and the venom in her tone was nothing to the hatred in her eyes. "You're the death of my husband!"

Immediately Cora and Ojay grabbed hold again to save Mary from collapse and keep her moving along, while Sam Henry paled before her accusation and was speechless to reply. Frozen around him, others became absolutely still. Front saw his mother clasp his father's hand and push him out into the flow of people now filing for the door. He had never felt such animosity before.

Relieved to reach outside, Front looked around at the crowd slowly dispersing and saw Goeff and Gordie standing not far off. He wanted to say something to the sons of the man who had died saving his father's life, but what? How could he give gratitude without offending? He couldn't. So walking over, he said the minimum the situation would allow.

"I'm sorry about your father."

Gordie didn't seem to hear, but Goeff was in no mood for sympathy. Not from the survivor's son. Too proud to take condolence from an enemy, he snarled a short reply.

"Don't be!" Then stalked away. The gall of anger was starting to feel good. Grievance was yielding a bitter satisfaction. As he savored the sullen joys of self-pity and resentment, Goeff found himself thirsting for more.

Feeling rebuffed, Front rejoined his parents, still holding hands, isolated, in social quarantine from the crowd of people who talked among themselves and attended Mary in a deliberate display of loyalty and blame intolerable to Estelle.

"We're leaving," she announced to Front, stung by the treatment they were receiving. Leading Sam to the car, she helped him in. This was all new to Front. Seeing his father, usually robust, act so shaken. Seeing his mother, usually indifferent, act so caring.

Arriving home, they acted this way as well. Rather than go their separate ways, his parents sat together on the couch in the living room, more mindful of each other than of him. So Front ambled off to his room to read, occasionally noticing the murmur of his parents talking and talking. What about, he idly wondered? With each other they didn't usually have much to say. Back to his book. He didn't know near death had brought his parents' marriage back to life.

Nor did they. Gratitude was all they knew. For just being alive. For having one another. Too much gratitude not to get renewal started. They couldn't stop the flood of conversation between them.

Sam was more than shaken.   He was wounded. Mary's accusation had drawn blood of guilt. He felt more responsibility than he could bear.

"I have so much to answer for," he confessed. "I could have gotten myself killed and would have if not for MacGregor, and I got him killed. Mary was right. Why do you suppose he rescued me?"

"I don't believe he did," answered Estelle, not arguing, not even offering comfort. "He wasn't trying to save you. He was there to see you drown."

"Stel!" Sam was shocked at her suggestion.   "You can't be serious! If he'd wanted to see me drown he had only to stay on the bank and watch."

"I know," Estelle agreed. "You're right. But so am I. Nothing you ever told me about the man would cause him to risk his life for yours. You had become his enemy. Mr. Detmer told you so himself."

Sam's good nature rebelled against this explanation. How could he think ill of the man who saved him?

"No, Stel. There must have been a reason!"

"Maybe there was," she persisted. "Maybe we just don't know."

But Sam could not let the matter go. Words were the only way he had to relieve the besetting pain. Over and over the experience he went, from the drowning to the funeral, what it meant and how it felt and how he felt about himself, Estelle just gently listening, getting to know her husband more deeply, he appreciating her receptiveness as he had not before.

That night all three began planning for their departure in another day. Back to work, back to school, back to living scheduled instead of free. Estelle and Front would start packing up next morning while Sam drove into town to pick up groceries for the trip home.

Under the watchful eye of Mrs. Detmer, Wally was managing the store. Cora was looking after Mary, Sam was told. On the way in he was greeted warmly by Mr. Detmer who waited to converse when he came out.

"Well Mr. D.," began Sam, "you warned me but I wouldn't listen. If I hadn't gone fishing when I shouldn't, MacGregor would be alive today."

"Probably so, Mr. Henry, probably so. But I was only guessing for the worst. You had no way of knowing, not for sure. Hindsight sounds wise enough, but it's blind to what's ahead. Best we can do is do the best we can. You played the contest hard. So did MacGregor. You lost and won. He won and lost. It wasn't anybody's fault. It was the competition."

"You don't hold it against me, do you Mr. D.?"

"No, Mr. Henry," the old man replied. "I've lived too long to see much good in blame."

"But the rest of the town?" asked Sam.

"Forgetting my take time, Mr. Henry. Give them time."

But it was about time Sam had been thinking, how many years of time were needed to forget his crime. Too many.

"I don't think I'll be coming back to Bishop's Place, Mr. D."

"No, Mr. Henry, I don't suppose you will. And there's another loss. Summers won't seem complete without you." Sadly spoken.

Sam gave a rueful smile back.

"My summers won't seem complete without you either Mr. D." He shook the old man's hand. "Goodbye."

"Goodbye Mr. Henry. Have a safe trip home." And Mr. Detmer settled back into the rocker, marking time, watching Sam drive off, watching life go on.

In his rear view mirror Sam saw the town grow smaller and recede from sight, then realized he better look where he was heading which he did, not noticing another car catch up with his and follow. As he parked at the bungalow, the second car pulled up behind.

"Sam!"

He turned around.

"Ojay, what brings you out this way?"

"You do," Ojay replied. "You and your family." She wasn't good at this and it felt awkward. "After how the contest went, I thought you might be leaving permanent. Was hoping you and the wife and boy would stop for breakfast on your way out of town. On the house. For old time's sake."

Sam felt a deeper warmth in this invitation than the simple words conveyed, the sum of all the summers of playful arguments and friendly insults, of sharing fishing news and fishing tips. How they had learned to express their liking for each other. Indirectly, but sincerely meant.

"Sounds great! Is six o'clock too early?" He knew it wasn't.

"Ain't no such hour too early for a fisherman," she retorted.

Sam laughed.

"Just so long as I don't have to wake you up."

And she laughed too as she drove off.

Inside the bungalow the hall was lined with boxes filled with books and clothes and fishing gear and food stuffs they hadn't used.

"Looks like you two got us about ready," Sam observed.

Estelle gave him a hug of welcome and he hugged her back. Front felt embarrassed. He almost liked it better when they didn't touch. Except it pleased him now they did.

Sam smiled at the look he was receiving from his son.

"What say you and I walk up to the bend in the river. Not to fish. To say goodbye."

"I'd like that." Front had not been back there since the night of their adventure with the great trout.

"We'll only be gone a little while, Stel." Promised Sam.

"Take your time. Enjoy yourselves." She hoped her husband might find some healing.

The trail through the woods soon brought them out on the river. Glancing downstream before heading up, Sam stopped short, startled by what he saw. Down below there was a fisherman Sam swore he recognized. He looked more closely. No, it wasn't. But it could have been.

"For a moment," he confided to Front, "I thought it was MacGregor. The same powerful motion. See how he forces the line forward when he casts. But it's Goeff. Growing up to be the spitting image of his father. Probably out fishing for the family dinner."

They turned upstream, detouring through the woods because the river, although fallen was still high, at last emerging above the rocky beach from which the boy had cast that memorable night. A broken log provided them a place to sit.

"Do you think he's still in there?" Front found the question irresistible to ask.

"Unless he got flooded out," Sam replied without thinking. What? As soon as he had said it a picture of the river flashed to mind, of a dark shape bobbing down the current. He ran the picture by again. "Unless the river was too much to fight and evicted him from home," he repeated aloud. Then silently, just to himself, 'and if that wasn't a log it could have been the reason. Stel was right! I'll have to tell Estelle. MacGregor would do anything to keep that fish from being caught.'

But Sam did not share this possibility with Front. He didn't want the boy connecting his release of the great trout to MacGregor's death. Instead, he half responded to his son's original question.

"I suspect that fish is in there somewhere, and always will be for you and me."

"Did you ever want to go back and fish for him again?" Front was curious.

"Oh no! I came closer to catching him then ever I wanted. Narrow escape. Lucky I was spared and I'm still grateful. A live challenge beats a dead trophy any day. How about you?"

"No," Front became serious. "I still love fishing, but I don't feel like doing it anymore. I guess I've changed."

"I guess you have."

"I feel a lot better now," confided Front. "It was hard for a while."

"Yes. It was hard watching you. Not being able to ease your pain. Even knowing the other side of loss is freedom is no comfort when all you see is what got left behind. It's been a struggle all right."

"I've been reading." Front brightened up. "That's helped."

"So I've been told."

"It's not exactly like fishing." Front didn't know how to describe the pleasure.

"Not exactly."

"But a person could learn to love it." Front wanted his father to know.

"They could." Sam could feel his son was on to something.

"How come you never told me about books?"

"Never been much of a reader, so it wasn't something I could recommend. I told you about fishing."

Now Front shared what was puzzling him.

"I've been wondering how a person goes about making up a story, thinking I'd like to try. Except I don't have any ideas."

"Maybe you do."

"No," Front felt downcast. "I've looked."

Sam wasn't so sure.

"Maybe you haven't searched in the right place, closest to home. Who knows, if the memories stir you strongly enough one day you might put your desire to make up stories and your love of fishing together and tell about this summer and the King of Trout."

Front dismissed the idea.

"That wouldn't work. People would never believe what I had to say."

Sam saw the point his son was missing.

"They wouldn't have to. That's the beauty of it, don't you see. A fishing story doesn't have to be true to be told, doesn't have to be believed to be enjoyed. It's like one of those flies we tie – just imitation and illusion wound around a hook. No fish in their right mind are going to bite for something so unlikely, yet they do. And although Ojay would argue against us, and does, you and I both know the artificial can be every bit as alluring as the real. Even more so. Now, just suppose you were going to spin such a tale, what kind of opening would you use to catch someone's interest?"

Front paused to consider this possibility, noticing a familiar sense of anticipation begin to build. He felt excited. Here was a new way to fish. For ideas.

"I think," he spoke at last, "I think I'd start right here by describing this pool and the great trout laying in it, waiting for something to eat."

"Sounds like a good beginning to me," encouraged Sam. "Why I can almost hear you telling it already."

THE END

BIOGRAPHY

Carl Pickhardt Ph.D. is a well-published author, graphic artist, and psychologist retired from thirty years of private counseling practice in Austin, Texas. He learned to fly fish as a child and believes that fishing is a metaphor for pursuing goals in life. You have to keep casting for what you want, persevere if nothing bites, and you might even hook what you are after. As one of the fishermen in *The Trout King* says: "There's much more to fishing than catching fish."

He is also the author of a popular blog about parenting teenagers for *Psychology Today: Surviving your Child's Adolescence* which has received over 13 million reads.

Information about his other books, and monthly articles about parenting and family, can be found on his website: www.carlpickhardt.com.

THE TROUT KING

More than a fisherman's tale, *The Trout King* is a story about fathers and sons, about boyhood and manhood, about the many meanings fishing holds for those who love it, and about how the unintended consequences of well-meaning choices can shape people's lives for good and ill.

The dramatic action unfolds over a summer contest in a small vacation community to determine the champion trout fisherman, "The Trout King," a competition that turns deadly serious when a rough-hewn local who has not been bested is challenged by a fly fishing purist who hates to lose.

www.ingramcontent.com/pod-product-compliance
Lightning Source LLC
Chambersburg PA
CBHW020441130626
46549CB00001B/247